Table of Contents

Grammar Genie 5

Who said Grammar was difficult? 7
    mail to: elena@masterlingua.gr 12
    http://www.boubouli.gr 12

The verbs "to be","can", "have" and "have got" 13

Subject Pronouns, Object Pronouns, Possessive Adjectives, Possessive Pronouns 19

Possessive Case-Genitive Case('S) 22

Reflexive Pronouns (myself, yourself, etc.) 25

PRESENT TENSES 26
  Simple Present 26
    Stative verbs: 32
    Verbs used both in progressive and non-progressive tenses: 33
  Present Continuous 34
  Present Perfect 37
    Present Perfect vs Present Perfect Continuous 41
    Have gone to/have been to/have been in: 41
    For/since: 42
  Present Perfect Continuous 43

PAST TENSES 44
  Past Simple 44
    Used to 45
    Would 45
  Past Continuous (Past Progressive) 46
    Stative verbs 50
  Past Perfect 52
  Past Perfect Continuous 55
    Past Perfect Continuous vs Present Perfect Continuous 57

FUTURE TENSES 58

- Future Continuous 60

PASSIVE VOICE 61
- Tenses of passive voice 67

CAUSITIVE 68
- Have /get something done 69
- Have someone do something 71
- Get someone to do something 72

CONDITIONALS 73
- Type 0 73
- Type 1 73
- Type 2 76
- Type 3 78
- Time and Condition Clauses 79
- Unreal Past Tenses with "Wish" = "If only" 81

INDIRECT SPEECH (REPORTED SPEECH) 82
- Indirect Questions (reported questions) 91
- Reporting the imperative (orders, requests, suggestions) ... 93
- POSITIVE IMPERATIVE 93

QUESTION TAGS 101
- Special Question Tags: 104
- Agreement to affirmative sentences 106
- Agreement to negative sentences 106
- Disagreement to affirmative sentences 107
- Disagreement to negative sentences 107

ADJECTIVES/ADVERBS 110

We use the adjective "bad" to describe emotions, feelings and states and the adverb "badly" to descrive actions: 117

THE COMPARATIVE AND SUPERLATIVE OF ADJECTIVES 118
- Adjectives that have irregular comparative and superlative forms: . 121

THE COMPARATIVE AND SUPERLATIVE OF ADVERBS 123
- Irregular adverbs: 125
- More comparisons: 126
- Agreement to affirmative sentences 127
- Agreement to negative sentences 128

Clauses of result 129
So-Such 129
Too/enough 131

Clauses of concession or contrast clauses 133

THE DEFINITE ARTICLE (THE) 138

THE INDEFINITE ARTICLE (A/AN) 143

COUNTABLE NOUNS 145

UNCOUNTABLE NOUNS 148
Plural collective nouns 152

QUANTIFIERS 153
A few vs few 153
A little vs little 153
A lot of/much/many 153
Both/both of 154
Some 155
Any 156
No 158
No 158

GERUND 160
Be used to 163
Get used to 163

THE INFINITIVE 164

BARE INFINITIVE 166

RELATIVE CLAUSES 169
Defining relative clauses 169
Non-defining relative clauses 172

MODAL VERBS 174
Modal infinitives 182
Helping verbs or auxiliary verbs 184

Irregular Verbs 186

Helen Boubouli, a foreign language teacher and entrepreneur with 30 years of experience teaching English as a second language, and a B.A in English and French from Worcester State College, is the creator of Grammar Genie.

Helen is convinced that learning can be enjoyable, creative and an interesting journey, and that grammar presented as art can motivate one to learn and equip one with valuable knowledge.

"I spent most of my teaching years writing and doing research on grammar points, and how best to present them to my students. This book is the result of thirty years of hard work that I must say I enjoyed every minute of it. Now is the time to share it with you and hope that you will benefit from it as much as I have. My students love it, and so will you."

Helen Boubouli   **Grammar Genie**

**Learn English
with**

**Grammar Genie
by Helen Boubouli**

Copyright © 2016

by Helen Boubouli

All rights reserved. No part of this publication may be reproduced, distributed, or transmitted in any form or by any means, including photocopying, recording, or other electronic or mechanical methods, without the prior written permission of the publisher, except in the case of brief quotations embodied in critical reviews and certain other noncommercial uses permitted by copyright law.

Helen Boubouli **Grammar Geni**e

Who said Grammar was difficult?
A self-study reference to grammar

A reference to **Beginning and Pre-intermediate** English grammar with clear examples and explanations aimed at students learning English as a second language, or native speakers of English wishing to learn the correct usage of the language. If you are **an English learner** and getting your message across is all you are interested in, then Grammar Genie is not for you. If you want more than just to be able to get your message across, Grammar Genie will show you the way in just 2 easy steps. The Grammar Genie makes it really easy to learn how to speak and write correct English.

You learn fast, easily, and without having to attend hundreds of hours of English lessons. It is designed for self-study, but it can also be used in the classroom. You learn grammar structures through lots of easy to understand examples.

Clever and brief grammar rules, and a lot of easy to learn examples of all the grammar structures.

Grammar Genie says that if you're learning English as a second language, you can learn the correct usage of grammar, both in spoken English, and in written English by following two easy steps:

Step 1 **STUDY:** You study a particular grammar structure.

Step 2 **REPEAT:** You repeat it many times to assimilate it. Learn it by heart if you can. Yes by heart. You learn one grammar structure at a time.

Repeat many times the particular grammar structure, and the examples that follow each structure to make sure you have assimilated it. It's important that you have a lot of repetition.

You repeat to yourself the examples of the particular structure that you are studying, and you learn by listening to your self repeating something many times. After all, isn't this the way you've learned your native language by hearing something many times. In less than six months you can learn to **use the English language correctly guaranteed**.

If you are a **native speaker,** you follow the same two steps, but you will need much less time to learn a structure. In less than two months you can learn to use grammar correctly in both spoken and written English guaranteed. The way the grammar is presented is so well-thought-of that it makes learning grammar easy, fun, and most of all fast for both learners of English as a second language and native speakers too. **Grammar is presented in the most innovative way ever.**

Learning English can be fun, and you can learn it on your own without having to attend classes.

Grammar Genie addresses all those who want to save time and money. My students love it, and so will you. They learn three structures a week on their own at home, and we spend the time in class doing oral work, listening, and drilling. Instead of spending endless hours talking about grammar, we use the grammar structures that we have studied in drilling and speaking in the classroom. You learn fast, yes, really fast. Whoever said that grammar is difficult should definitely reconsider.

Try learning with the Grammar Genie.

Helen Boubouli   **Grammar Genie**

If you are an English teacher, Grammar Genie does all the work for you.

If you are an **English teacher,** you can use Grammar Genie as reference to teach grammar. It's really easy to teach, and your students learn easily.

Grammar is a resource which enables you to get your message across correctly.

The aim of Grammar Genie is to discourage students and teachers from seeing grammar as a set of rules, to help them to develop a richer understanding of the relationship between language and context, and to view grammar as a resource for getting their message across using the correct language.

Although Grammar Genie is designed for self-study, it can also be used as reference in the classroom. It's a unique grammar reference for ESL/EFL teachers, and for ESL/EFL students from Beginning to Intermediate levels.

Making grammar mistakes is attributed to not knowing the correct usage of the language. The Grammar Genie shows you how to improve both your speaking and writing skills easily, painlessly, and effortlessly. The Grammar Genie is a pioneer in the way grammar is presented.

Don't wait. Learn English with this unique and most clever method ever, now.

mail to: elena@masterlingua.gr

http://www.boubouli.gr

Helen Boubouli   **Grammar Geni**e

The verbs "to be","can", "have" and "have got

Affirmative forms of the verb "to be":

Subject Pronouns	Full Form	Contracted Form
I	am	'm
you	are	're
he/she/it	is	's
we	are	're
you	are	're
they	are	're

Tim and Tina are good friends.

They are from Greece.

Negative Forms of the verb to be:

Subject Pronouns	Full Form	Contracted Form
I	am not	'm not
you	are not	aren't
he/she/it	is not	isn't
we	are not	aren't
you	are not	aren't
they	are not	aren't

I am not French

John and Mary are not American.

Helen Boubouli   **Grammar Genie**

Interrogative forms of the verb to be:

Am	I?
Are	you?
Is	he/she/it?
Are	we?
Are	you?
Are	they?

-Is Ann French?

-No, she isn't. She's American. What about Maria? Is she American, too?

-Yes, she is. She is American.

Affirmative and Negative forms of the verb "can":

Subject Pronouns	Affirmative	Negative long	Negative short
I	can	cannot	can't
you	can	cannot	can't
he/she/it	can	cannot	can't
we	can	cannot	can't
you	can	cannot	can't
they	can	cannot	can't

Helen Boubouli   **Grammar Geni**e

Simple Present affirmative

She can drive a car.

John can speak Spanish.

Simple Present negative

I can't write a letter.

They can't speak English.

Interrogative forms of the verb "can":

can	I?
can	you?
can	he/she/it?
can	we?
can	you?

Simple Present interrogative

Can you make a cup of tea, please.

Can you be quiet!

Can I smoke in this room?(permission)

Affirmative and Negative forms of the verb "have"

Subject Pronouns	Affirmative	Negative long	Negative short
I	have	do not have	don't have
You	have	do not have	don't have
He/She/It	has	does not have	doesn't have
We	have	do not have	don't have
You	have	do not have	don't have
They	have	do not have	don't have

Simple Present affirmative

She has a car.

Simple Present negative

John doesn't have a car.

We don't have any money.

Helen Boubouli   **Grammar Genie**

Interrogative forms of the verb "have":

Do	I	have?
Do	you	have?
Does	He/she/it	have?
Do	we	have?
Do	you	have?
Do	they	have?

Simple Present interrogative

Does Paul have curly hair?

Do you have a computer?

Affirmative and Negative forms of the "have got"

Subject Pronouns	Affirmative	Negative long	Negative short
I	have got	have not got	haven't got
You	have got	have not got	haven't got
He/She/It	has got	has not got	hasn't got
We	have got	have not got	haven't

			got
You	have got	have not got	haven't got
They	have got	have not got	haven't got

Simple Present affirmative

She has got a car.

Simple Present negative

John hasn't got a car.

We haven't got any money.

Interrogative forms of "have got":

Have	I	**got**
Have	you	got
Has	He/she/it	got
Have	we	got
Have	you	got
Have	they	got

Helen Boubouli   **Gramm**a**r Geni**e

Simple Present interrogative

Has Paul got curly hair?

Have you got a computer?

Subject Pronouns, Object Pronouns, Possessive Adjectives, Possessive Pronouns

Personal Subject Pronouns

Pronouns are words we use **as subjects before verbs** instead of full nouns.

-Where is Steve?

-**He**'s at work.

Singular	Plural
I	We
You	You
He	They
She	
It	

I like your shoes.

You are pretty.

She is my friend

He has beautiful eyes.

It is raining

We live in England.

You are my friends.

They come from London.

Object Pronouns

We use object pronouns:

after verbs as the object of the verb

Can you help **me** please?

I like **you.**

She doesn't know **him.**

We saw **them** yesterday, but they didn't see us.

after prepositions

She is waiting **for me.**

Give it **to her**

Why are you looking **at me?**

Don't give it **to them.**

Possessive adjectives

We use possessive adjectives:

to show something belongs to somebody

That's **our house.** **My car** is very old.

Helen Boubouli					**Grammar Genie**

for relations and friends

My mother is a doctor. How old is your sister?

for parts of the body

He's broken **his leg.**

I'm washing **my hair.**

Possessive Pronouns

We can use a possessive pronoun **to replace a noun phrase:**

Is that Mary's pen?

No, it's [my pen]= No, it's **mine.**

Whose bag is this?

Is it [your bag]? =Is it **yours?**

Her bag is red

[my bag]is black. = **Mine** is black.

We can use possessive pronouns after "of"

We can say:
Kate is one of my friends. **or** Kate is **a friend of mine**

or
I am one of Kate's friends.
  or
I am a friend of Kate's
       but not
~~I am a friend of Kate~~

Possessive Case-Genitive Case('S)

The possessive case or the genitive case is when we add **apostrophe S ('s)** to show possession, that something belongs to another or a type of relationship between things.

Singular nouns: add 's (apostrophe S)

John**'s** car

Your **father's** boss

John**'s** house was broken into last night. (= the car of John)

My mother**'s** house is next to the post office. (= the house of my mother)

They had a really good time at **Steve's party** last night.

People's names that end in "s" you can write (') or ('s).

Charles' job was on the line.

or

Charles's job was on the line.

Classical or religious names: add ' (only the apostrophe)

Jesu**s'** disciples went out to teach the people.

Sophocle**s'** Antigone is a tragedy written before 441 BC.

Plural nouns ending in -s : only add the apostrophe ' (without the s)

The two brother**s'** business was established 20 years ago. (= the business of the two brothers)

The player**s'** boots were dirty after the game. (= the boots of the players)

The girl**s'** dresses had to be shortened.

My parent**s'** house was broken into.

The boy**s'** toys were under the bed.

Plural nouns not ending in –s: add **'s**

She got a job in the **children's** hospital ward.

The women**'s** house was broken into.

Possessive nouns as part of a phrase

The **King of Ithaca's** name was Odysseus..

I took **someone else's** home by mistake.

If there are two owners of something, we add 's to the final name:

John and **Tim's** house is modern.

But, if each person owns a house, then add 's to both names:

John's and **Tim's** houses **are** modern. (The verb is in plural form, because there are two houses.)

We can use the possessive without a noun after it if the meaning is clear:

Her house is cleaner than **Mary's.** (=**Mary's house**)

We had dinner **at Kate's** last Saturday. (=**Kate's house**)

Whose books are these? There **Helen's**. (=**Helen's books**)

Helen Boubouli   **Grammar Genie**

Reflexive Pronouns (myself, yourself, etc.)

Reflexive Pronouns show that **the action of the verb affects the person or thing performing the action.** They refer back to the subject pronouns. Reflexive pronouns end in **-self or –selves:**

The cat washed **herself** carefully with her tongue.

Subject Pronouns	Reflexive Pronouns
I	Myself
You	Yourself
He	Himself
She	Herself
It	Itself
We	Ourselves
You	Yourselves
They	Themselves

Julie is always **looking at herself** in the mirror.

The boy hurt himself while playing.

She made the cake herself

Reflexive pronouns + by meaning alone:

Jane is a baby, she is too small to eat **by herself**

Why don't you go **by yourself?**

PRESENT TENSES

Simple present

STRUCTURE

In the third person singular of regular verbs: **verb +s/es**

My mother read**s** the news paper every day.

Affirmative	Interrogative	Negative	Short form
I play	Do I play?	I do not play	I don't play
You play	Do you play?	You do not play	You don't play
He/she/it plays	Does he/she/it play?	He/she/it does not play	He/she/it doesn't play
We play	Do we play?	We do not play	We don't play
You play	Do you play?	You do not play	You don't play
They play	Do they play?	They do not play	They don't play

The verb **"have"** is **irregular in the third person singular:**

I always have coffee in the morning.

He always has supper at six o'clock.

Helen Boubouli   **Grammar Genie**

Affirmative	Short form	Negative	Short form	Interrogative
I have	I've	**I do not have**	I don't have	**Do I have?**
You have	You've	**You do not have**	You don't have	**Do you have?**
He/she/it has	He's/she's/it's	**He/she/it does not have**	He/she/it doesn't have	**Does he/she/it have?**
We have	We've	**We do not have**	We don't have	**Do we have?**
You have	You've	**You do not have**	You don't have	**Do you have?**
They have	They've	**They do not have**	They don't have	**Do they have?**

The verb **"be" is irregular** and the interrogative and negative is formed with the same verb:

Gus is a very happy boy.

Helen is not here today.

Is john here?

Affirma Tive	Short Form	Negative	Short Form	Interrogative
I am	I'm	**I am not**	I'm not	**Am I?**
You are	You're	**I am not**	You're not	**Are you?**
He/she/it is	He/she/it's	**He/she/it is not**	He's/she's/it's not or He/she/it isn't	**Is he/she/it?**
We are	We're	**We are not**	We're not or We aren't	**Are we?**
You are	You're	**You are not**	You're not or You aren't	**Are you?**
They are	They're	**They are not**	They're not or They aren't	**Are they?**

Helen Boubouli **Grammar Genie**

If a verb ends in **ss, z, sh, ch, o** we use **"es"** instead of "s" in the third person singular:

She tea**ch**es English.

He always mi**ss**es the school bus.

Mary bru**sh**es her teeth every morning.

John wat**ch**es TV every evening.

Helen g**oes** to the supermarket every Friday.

If a verb ends in consonant+y we change the "y" to an "i" and add "es":

Stu**dy**⮕She studi**es** very hard.

Fly⮕ Tom is a pilot. He fli**es** a plane.

In interrogative, negative sentences and short answers of regular verbs we use: **do/does:**

-**Do** you know why they're late?

-No, **I don't.**

-**Does** she speak English?

-Yes, **she does.**

Short forms of all verbs in the negative: **don't/doesn't**

I **don't** like tennis.

My daughter **doesn't have a computer.**

Short forms of the verb "to be": I'm, you're, he's, she's, it's, we're, you're, they're

Anthony is a good kid, but **he's** always late for school.

Helen is very smart. **She's** good in everything she does.

Short answers of all verbs in the present: I, you, we, they do/don't/ She, he, it does/doesn't

Do you know her? Yes, **I do.** No**, I don't.**

Does she know us? Yes, **She does.** No, **she doesn't.**

Short answers of the verb "to be" in the present: I am, you, we, they are/ he, she, it is

I am not, you, we, they are not, he, she, it, is not

Are you happy? Yes, **I am.** No, **I am not.**

Yes, **we are.** No, **we are not.**

Is she arrogant? Yes, **she is.** No, **she is not.**

USE

We use simple present for:

present habits

I have breakfast at 7:00 a.m.

repeated actions usually with frequency adverbs (usually, often, frequently, rarely, seldom, etc)

The family always has lunch together on Sundays.

general truths

It rarely snows in Southern Greece.

Helen Boubouli **Grammar Genie**

laws of nature
The sun sets in the west.

The moon moves around the earth.

timetables and schedules in the near future
Our dancing class **begins at 6:00** p.m.

I go to work at 7:00 a.m.

states with STATIVE VERBS
I love chocolate.

I hate french fries

sports commentaries and reviews of novels, film, plays, etc.
Beckham scores and **the audience scream** with joy.

narrations and jokes even when we are talking about the past.
Tom Hunks **plays** Professor Robert Langdon in, The Da Vinci Code.

newspaper headlines
Snow storm stops traffic.

Frequency adverbs and time expressions used with simple present:

(every day/week/month/year/Monday/Tuesday etc), (always, often, usually, sometimes, never, seldom, rarely), (once a day/ week/ month/ year), (twice a day/ week/ month), (on Mondays/ Tuesdays, etc.)

Stative verbs:

Action verbs express what a person does. **Stative verbs** express states which continue over a period of time, rather than actions and **are not usually used in continuous tenses.** Here is a list of the most frequently used stative verbs:

Senses	hear, see, smell, taste, feel, sound
Possession	have, own want, contain, belong to
Emotions	like, love, enjoy, hate, dislike, want, need, prefer, hope, wish, feel, forgive
Opinion	think, believe, suppose, agree, understand, seem
Measurement	weigh, cost, measure, equal
mental states	know, remember, forget, mean, look(appear), mind
other stative verbs	decide, resemble, tend, conclude, perceive, appreciate, recognize, be(exist)

Helen Boubouli   **Grammar Genie**

> **Note:** Stative verbs are not usually used in continuous tenses because they are not action verbs.

Verbs used both in progressive and non-progressive tenses:

When the following stative verbs are used in progressive (continuous) tenses, they have a different meaning than when they are used in non-progressive tenses:

Non-progressive	Progressive(continuous)
"have" with the meaning of possession	**"have"** enjoy one self
"see" look with the eyes	**"see"** meet or date sm
"think" believe	**"think"** someone's thoughts
"feel" describing someone's mood	**"feel"** touch
"smell" talking about how something smells	**"smell"** using one's nose to undersand how something smells
"be" describing how you are	**"be"** behaving in a certain way
"appear" seem	**"appear"** give a performance, give a speech, etc

Present continuous

Affirmative	Short	Negative	Short	Interrogative
I am playing	I'm	I am not playing	I'm not	Am I playing?
You are playing	You're	You are not playing.	You're not (you aren't)	Are you playing?
He/she/it is playing	He's/ she's	He/she/it is not playing	He's/ she's/ it's not (He/she/it isn't)	Is he/she/it playing?
We are playing	We're	We are not playing	We're not (we aren't)	Are we playing?
You are playing	You're	You are not playing	You're not (you aren't)	Are you playing?
They are playing	They're	They are not playing	They're not (they aren't)	Are they playing?

Helen Boubouli **Grammar Genie**

Structure

no short forms in the interrogative:

Are you playing?

Use

We use present continuous, also called present progressive for:

something happening **now**(at present):

I'm talking to you.

The kids are studying right now.

Turn the television down. The kids are sleeping.

longer actions in progress at the present moment(now), but not necessarily happening at the moment of speaking(now):

I'm living in Athens.

Romy is studying to become a lawyer.

I'm still writing this grammar book.

future plans and arrangements in the near future:

When are you coming home?

I'm working next week.

Expressions used with present continuous:

Now, at the moment (of speaking,) look! listen!, right now, still, currently, today, tonight, this week, this month, tomorrow, on Monday, Tuesday, etc, next week.

Note: Stative verbs are not usually used in continuous tenses because they are not action verbs.

Present perfect

Structure

Affirmative:	Subject	+	Has/have	+	Past participle of the main verb
Negative	Subject	+	has/have not	+	past participle of the main verb
Interrogative	Have/has	+	Subject	+	past participle of the main verb

I have always loved you.

I have not been to Egypt yet.

Have you seen Mary recently?

Most past participles end in -ed. There is a long list, however, of irregular past participles at the end of the book that must be learned by heart.

Affirmative	Affirmative short	Negative	Negative short	Interrogative
I have loved	I've	**I have not loved**	I haven't	**Have I loved?**
You have loved	you've	**You have not loved**	You haven't	**Have you loved?**
He has loved	he's	**He has not loved**	He hasn't	**Has he loved?**
She has loved	She's	**She has not loved**	She hasn't	**Has she loved?**
It has loved	It's	**It has not loved**	It hasn't	**Has it loved?**
We have loved	We've	**We have not loved**	We haven't	**Have we loved?**
You have loved	You've	**You have not loved**	You haven't	**Have you loved?**
They have loved	They've	They have not loved	They haven't	Have they loved?

40

Use

We use the present perfect:

for an action that happened at an **indefinite/unspecified time in the past.** We are not interested in when the action happened, but in what happened.

I have told you what she said.

Have you ever ridden a horse?

for an action that happened in the past, but **has an effect on the present**

I **haven't seen my parents** for three years.
(=The last time I saw my parents was three years ago).

for an action that started in the past and is still going on.(often with **"for"/ "since"**)

I have worked as a teacher for 24 years.
(=I started working as a teacher 24 years ago, and I'm still working as a teacher.)

I have lived in Greece for 27 years.
(=I came to Greece 27 years ago, and I'm still living here.)

for an action that was repeated several times in the past with emphasis on quantity.**(usually with twice/three times, etc/many/several times etc.)**

I have seen this film **several times.**

I have been to Paris **three times.**

after:**This is / it is / he is+ SUPERLATIVE + Present perfect**

This is the best book (that) **I have ever read.**

It is the most interesting lecture **I have ever attended.**

after: It is / this is the first /second/last/only time+ **Present Perfect**

It is **the first time** I have (that) ever said that.

> **Time expressions and prepositional phrases used with** interrogative and negative sentences),**:**
> for, since, how long, recently, lately, yet (at the end of just, never, ever (with interrogative sentences), already, so far(beginning or end of a sentence), up to now, today, this week/month/year, all day/week/morning, etc.

Have you seen John **recently**?

How long have you been studying Eglish**?**

Have you called home **yet?**

We do not use the Present Perfect with definite time expressions such as **yesterday, last week, two months ago, etc**. We use simple past instead:

I **came** to Greece 30 years ago.

Helen Boubouli   **Grammar Genie**

Present perfect vs Present perfect continuous

Present perfect and present perfect continuous are used interchangeably when talking about **an action that started in the past, and continuous into the present** with verbs of movement such as live, work, etc

I **have lived** in Greece since 1980.

I **have been living** in Greece since 1980.

Time expressions, usually come between has/have and the main verb. However, **yet** comes at the end of a sentence, **so far** comes at the beginning or end of a sentence, and **ever** is used in questions:

I have **never** been to Australia.

Have you been to Rome **yet?**

So far we have only learned present tenses.

We have only learned present tenses **so far**.

Have you **ever** been to Rome?

Have gone to/have been to/have been in:

Helen **has gone** to Egypt.(She hasn't come back yet).

Helen **has been to** Egypt.(She has come back).

Helen **has been in** Egypt for five years.(That's where she lives now).

For/since:

For+period of time:
(for 5 days/months/years/weeks/minutes etc.)

I **haven't talked** to him for months.

Since+specific time
(since yesterday/Monday/1990/last week etc.):

I haven't talked to him since last week.

Since + simple past but Present perfect + since:

I **haven't talked** to Henry since he moved to New york.

It's year's/months/7 weeks/etc., since someone did something:

It's such a long time since I last saw you.

It's(has) been year's/months/4 weeks/etc, since someone did something:

It's (has) been a long time since I last went on vacation.

Helen Boubouli   Grammar Genie

Present perfect continuous
Structure

Affirmative:	Subject	+	Has/have been	+	Verb	+	ING
Negative:	Subject	+	has/have	+	not	+	been	+	ing
Interrogative:	Has/have	+	subject	+	been	+	verb	+	ing

I **have been writing letters** to him all these years.

I **have not been sleeping** well lately.

How long **have you exercising?**

Use:

We use present perfect continuous :

for an action that **started** at an unspecified(indefinite) **time in the past and continues in the present:**

I **have been working** on this book for three years

I **have been sleeping** for twelve hours.

for an action that started in the past but **whose results we can see in the present:**

(we have evidence in the present time that something has been happening).

Your eyes are red. Have you been crying?

You look really tired. Have you been working all night again?

> **Expressions used with present perfect continuous:**
> For, since, all day/week/morning, lately, how long

PAST TENSES
Past Simple

Structure:
Most verbs in the past tense end in – ed. There is, however, a long list of irregular verbs at the end of the book that must be learned by heart.

Use:
We use simple past:
for an action that **happened** and finished **at a definite(specific) time in the past** even if the speaker doesn't mention the exact time. We are more interested in when the action happened, and not so much in what happened.

I **had** fun at the **party last night.**

to express **past routines and habits.** It has the same meaning as "used to"

When I was a child **I woke up early** in the morning to watch cartoons.

Helen Boubouli   **Grammar Genie**

for **past actions happening one after the other**

When I was in school, **I woke up early** in the morning; **I took a shower**, had breakfast, brushed my teeth and **left for school.**

> **Time expressions used with simple past:**
> a week ago, five days ago, last week/month/year, yesterday, the other day, on Monday, in 1980, in June, in the past, etc.

Used to + bare infinitive ⮕ past habits/facts/states

Used to describes **past habits (actions)** that do not happen any more, **facts** and **states** that are no longer true.

Did John use to drink when he was younger? ▸ habit.

I used to like school. ▸ state (I don't like school any more.)

When I was little **I used to hate** spinach. ▸ state

I used to believe in God. ▸ state

He used to be smart. ▸ state

I used to live in America. ▸ fact

I used to be a good student. ▸ state

Would (always, rarely, seldom, occasionally, constantly, often, never) + **bare infinitive ⟹ past habits /not facts or states,**
and therefore is not used with stative verbs such as like, hate, enjoy, love, believe, remember etc.
With stative verbs we use **"used to"** instead:

✓**I would/used to wake up** early in the morning when I was in school. (**past habit**)

x I ~~would like~~ school. (**state**)

✓I **used to like** school. (**state**)

Would has no interrogative form. We use **used to** instead:

✓**Did you use to wake up** early in the morning?

x Would you wake up early in the morning?

Past Continuous (Past Progressive)
Affirmative

Subject	Auxiliary verb (was/were)	Main verb +ing	
I	**was**	**listening**	to music.
You	**were**	**watching**	TV.
He/she/it	**was**	**talking**	on the phone.
We	**were**	**dancing**	all night.
You	**were**	**sleeping.**	------------
They	**were**	**playing.**	------------

48

Helen Boubouli　　　　　**Grammar Genie**

Negative

Subject.	Auxiliary verb	Not	Main verb+ing	
I	was	not	listening	to you.
You	were	not	working	last night.
He/she/it	was	not	making	noise.
We	were	not	eating	--------
You	were	not	swimming	-------
They	were	not	driving	-------

Interrogative

Auxiliary verb	Subject	Main verb+ing	
Was	I	playing?	
Were	you	mowing	the lawn?
Was	he/she/it	sleeping?	
Were	we	playing?	----------
Were	you	typing?	an essay?
Were	they	thinking?	

short forms: wasn't/weren't in the negative

I **wasn't** singing in the shower.

He **wasn't** sleeping.

You **weren't** having coffee in the afternoon.

no short forms in the affirmative and interrogative

I was jogging in the park when I saw a huge dog.

Was he sleeping when you called?

Use

We use past continuous:

to emphasize **the duration of an action** that took place at a particular or specific time **in the past:**

-What **were you doing** on Sunday morning?

-I **was sleeping** of course. What else would I be doing on a Sunday Morning.

to express a long action interrupted by a shorter one. We use simple past to refer to the short action:

I **was ironing** when you **fell down** the stairs.

While I **was ironing**, you **fell** down the stairs.

I **was sleeping** when the telephone **rang.**

Helen Boubouli   **Grammar Geni**e

to express two actions happening at the same time in the past with "when" or "while":

I **was watching** TV **while** you **were talking** on the phone.

to express frequently repeated actions in the past annoying to the speaker with "always":

She **was always telling** lies.

> **Time expressions used with past continuous:**
> while, when, as:

As/while we were waking home, it started to rain.

Stative verbs

Action verbs express what a person does. **Stative verbs** express states continue over a period of time, rather than actions and **are not usually used in continuous tenses.**

Here is a list of the most frequently used stative verbs:

> **Stative verbs are not used in the past continuous:**

Senses	hear, see, smell, taste, feel, sound
Possession	have, own want, contain, belong to
Emotions	like, love, enjoy, hate, dislike, want, need, prefer, hope, wish, feel, forgive
Opinion	think, believe, suppose, agree, understand, seem
Measurement	weigh, cost, measure, equal
mental states	know, remember, forget, mean, look(appear), mind
other stative verbs	decide, resemble, tend, conclude, perceive, appreciate, recognize, be(exist)

Helen Boubouli   **Grammar Genie**

Verbs used both in progressive and non-progressive tenses

When the following stative verbs are used in progressive tenses, they have a different meaning than when they are used in non-progressive tenses:

Non-Progressive	Progressive (Continous)
"have" with the meaning of possession	**"have"** enjoy one self
"see" look with the eyes	**"see"** meet or date someone
"think" believe	**"think"** someone's thoughts
"feel" describing someone's mood	"feel" touch
"smell" talking about how something smells	**"smell"** using one's nose to understand **how** something smells
"be" describing how you are	**"be"** behaving in a certain way
"appear" seem	**"appear"** give a performance, give a speech, **etc**

Past Perfect

Past perfect is used:

for an action **that happened and was completed in the past**

Jane couldn't walk because she **had broken** her leg.

to describe **an action that happened in the past before another past action**

I **had spent** all my money when I saw this really nice pair of shoes on sale.(=first I spent all my money and then I saw this really nice pair of shoes).

I **had already left** the house when you came to see me.(=first I left and then you came.)

AFFIRMATIVE

Subject	had	past participle of the main verb		
I	had	talked	to him	earlier.
You	had	seen	her	before the accident.
He/she/it	had	had	been there	before.
We	had	answered	the phone	when it went dead.
You	had	left	the	when the

Helen Boubouli   **Grammar Genie**

			house	burglary occurred.
They	**had**	**finished**	**supper**	before I came home.

NEGATIVE

Subject	had	not	past participle of the main verb	
I	**had**	**not**	**talked**	to her.
You	**had**	**not**	**seen**	her.
He/she/it	**had**	**not**	**been**	there.
We	**had**	**not**	**answered**	the phone.
You	**had**	**not**	**left**	the house.
They	**had**	**not**	**finished**	yet.

Interrogative

Had	subject	past participle of the main verb	
Had	I	talked	to her?
Had	you	seen	her?
Had	he/she/it	been	there?
Had	we	answered	the phone?
Had	you	left	the house?
Had	they	finished	finished?

Time expressions used with past perfect:
By the time, by, by then, already, when, after, before, never, just, for, since, yet

By the time I got home, my roommate had already done the house work.(=first my roommate did the house work, and then I went home.)

1st action ➲ my roommate did the housework.

2nd action ➲ I went home.

By midnight, I had finished studying.(=I finished studying before midnight.)

Helen Boubouli   **Grammar Genie**

Past Perfect Continuous Affirmative

Subject	had	been	verb + ing		
I	had	been	working	**as a teacher**	before I moved here.
You	had	been	living	**in America**	when I first saw you.
He/she/it	had	been	lying	**to me**	for years before I found out.
We	had	been	talking	**on the phone**	when the phone rang.
You	had	been	swimming	**in the pool**	when I came.
They	had	been	sitting	**in the living room**	all evening.

57

Past perfect continuous is used:

to emphasize the continuity of an action before another past action

They won the dancing competition because **they had been practicing** really hard all year.

to express a **past action which had visible results in the past**

Her eyes were red because **she had been crying** all day.

Time expressions used with past perfect continuous: for, since, all day, night, week, month, year, how long

When my great grand parents moved to America they **had been married for** nearly fifty years.

They didn't want to move. They **had lived/been living** in Ireland **all their life.**

He was a wonderful pianist. He **had been playing** the piano **since** he was a teenager.

Helen Boubouli Grammar Genie

Past Perfect Continuous vs Present Perfect Continuous

Present Perfect Continuous for an action with **visible results in the present:**

I **am** late because **I have been working** all day.

Past Perfect Continuous for an action with **visible results in the past:**

I **was** late because **I had been working** all day.

FUTURE TENSES

Future forms
(Simple future(will)/going to/present continuous/simple present)

Simple future(will)	For a decision made at the moment of speaking:	It's too dark. I'll turn on the light. It's cold. I'll close the window.
	For a promise:	I'll buy you some ice cream if you behave, children. Don't worry mum, I'll drive carefully. Trust me, I won't tell anyone what you told me.
	For a prediction after: **be afraid, believe, expect, think, hope, certainly, sure, perhaps, maybe, probably**	I'm afraid, he will be late for dinner. He will probably get the job. I believe, that this will be a good year for us.

Helen Bouboulli   **Gra**m**ar Gen**ie

	To express willingness to do something:	I'll help you find a dress for your prom. You study for your exam and I'll do your house work.
	To express refusal to do something:	I won't lie to your parents for you.
Be going to:	For an intention/plan: (used in informal style)	I'm going to do graduate studies.
Present continuous:	For a future plan:	I'm leaving for Hong Kong on Monday. I'm coming to see you soon.
Simple present:	For timetables:	The plane takes off at 7:00 pm tomorrow. What time does the bus arrive in Boston? My lesson starts at 5:00 pm tomorrow. The stores are open on the last Sunday before Christmas.

** Note: "Will" is also used to make a request.
Will you help me set the table?

Future Continuous

Affirmative:	subject	+	will be	+	ing		
Negative:	subject	+	will	+	not be	+	ing
Interrogative:	will	+	be	+	ing		

We use future continuous:

to emphasize the duration of a future action

Tomorrow at this hour **I will be lying** on the beach in Myconos.

When you wake up tomorrow morning, **I will still be flying** to Australia.

to make polite requests about somebody's intentions

Will you be helping out at the charity ball this weekend?

When **will we be seeing** you again?

Helen Boubouli					**Gram**m**ar Geni**e

PASSIVE VOICE

In passive voice one is usually not interested in who performed the action but in the action itself:

Active voice ➲ The workers **are building** a garage.

Passive voice ➲ A garage **is being built.**

In passive voice:

a) The **object** in active voice **becomes the subject** of the sentence in passive voice.

b) We put **the verb to be** in **the same tense as the tense of the main verb** in active .

c) We add **the past participle of the main verb.**

d) **The agent**, however, many times not necessary **is expressed with(by).**

Active voice ➲ **The workers built a garage.**
		(Subject +Simple Past+object)

Passive voice ➲ **A garage was built by the workers.** (subject +past participle +agent)

By is omitted when the subject is not necessary, important unknown or obvious:

My hair **is washed** two times a week. (One understands who washes it.)

The house **has been cleaned.** (one is not interested in who cleaned the house..)

The car **was washed.**

My room **will be painted.**

The passive is usually used:

in more formal and spoken English:

The referee must inform the players of the cancellation of the game.(informal)

The players **must be informed** of the cancellation of the game. (formal)

in newspaper headlines, newspaper reports, academic and scientific writing:

The robbers **were caught** at dawn....

Helen Boubouli **Grammar Genie**

in informal English with **get+ past participle:**

Nicky **got punished** for lying to her mum.(She was punished.)

Some students **got caught** cheating on the test.(They were caught.)

to announce an accident with get+past participle:

The athlete **got his knee injured**. (He injured his knee.)

I got my finger cut. (I injured my finger.)

More on Passive voice
The passive with two objects

When we have two objects, a personal indirect object and a noun direct object, we usually change the personal indirect object into a subject pronoun, and place it at the beginning of the sentence to form the passive:

The cashier **gave me** a refund. ⮕active

   (me:personal indirect object)

I was given a refund by the cashier. ⮕passive

   (I:subject pronoun)

The noun direct object can also be used at the beginning of the sentence to form the passive for emphasis on that action:

The cashier gave me **a refund**. ⮕active
   (a refund:noun direct object)

A refund was given to me by the cashier. ⮕ passive
(a refund:subject noun)

Let/allow:

The verb **let** becomes **allow** in passive voice:

Active	Passive
The police **let the criminal go**.	The criminal **was allowed** to go.

Make/see/help/hear:

The verbs **make, see, help, hear +bare infinitive in active** voice become **make, see, help, hear+ full infinitive in passive** voice:

Active voice	Passive voice
My boss **made** me work over time.	I **was made** to work over time.
Helen **helped** Maria do her homework.	Maria **was helped** to do her homework.
I **saw** him leave the room.	He **was seen** to leave the room.

Verbs which are followed by a preposition carry the **preposition right after the verb** in passive voice:

Active voice	Passive voice
I am looking into the matter.	The matter is being looked **into.**

With/By:

> Using with and by in passive voice. **"By" is used for the person who or what performs the action**, **and** "with" **is used for the object used to perform the action:**

I was told **by** my professor that my test was excellent.

Many people were killed **by** the car crash.

He was shot **with** a shot gun.

He was stabbed **with** a knife.

68

Tenses of passive voice

Active voice	Passive voice
The scientist does **experiments.**	Experiments **are done** (by the scientist.)
The scientist is doing **experiments.**	Experiments **are being** done.
The scientist has done **experiments.**	Experiments **have been** done.
The scientist has been doing **experiments.**	-----------------------------
The scientist did **experiments.**	Experiments **were** done.
The scientist was doing **experiments.**	Experiments **were being** done.
The scientist had done **experiments.**	Experiments **had been** done.
The scientist will do **experiments.**	Experiments will be done.
The scientist is going to do **experiments.**	Experiments **are going to be** done.
The scientist might/may/can/should **do experiments.**	Experiments **might/may/ can/should be** done.

We **do not use passive constructions** for present perfect continuous, past perfect continuous, future continuous and future perfect continuous.

CAUSITIVE

The causative expresses an action performed by **someone else.** Someone else does something for you:

Passive causative form: There is no agent(by) in the passive form.

Have/get something done
Subject+Have/get (in the appropriate tense) + noun+the past participle of the verb)

Once every two months the hairdresser cuts my hair.
Once every two months **I have my hair cut**.(causitive)
(have +noun +past participle)

Get is a more informal construction:

Once every two months **I get my hair cut**.(**more informal causative)**
(get + noun + past participle)

Helen Boubouli **Grammar Genie**

Tenses of causative (passive causative)
Have /get something done

Simple present:	I have/get my hair cut.
Present continuous:	I'm having/getting my hair cut.
Present perfect :	I have had/ gotten my hair cut.
Present perfect continuous:	I have been having /getting my hair cut.
Simple past:	I had/got my hair cut.
Past perfect:	I had /gotten my hair cut.
Past perfect continuous:	I had been having/getting my hair cut.
Past continuous:	I was having/getting my hair cut.
Simple future:	I will have/get my hair cut.
Future continuous:	I will be having/getting my hair cut.
Future perfect continuous:	I will have been having/getting my hair cut.
Going to:	I am going to have/get my hair cut.
Modals:	I can, may, might, etc have/get my hair cut.

The causative is also used to state that **somebody does something to you:**

I **had my house broken into.** (=Somebody broke into my house.)

I **had my car crashed.** (=Somebody crashed my car.)

Active causative form: This construction is usually used when giving instructions. There is an agent in the active form.

> Have someone **do** something (=ask someone to do something)
>
> Get someone **to do** something (=ask someone to do something)
>
> Once every two months I **have the hairdresser cut** my hair.

Get is a more informal construction than have:

Once every two months I **get the hairdresser to cut** my hair.

I **got my mum to clean** my room.

Helen BoubouliGrammar Genie

Tenses of causative (active causative)

Have someone do something

Simple present: I have my hairdresser cut my hair.
Present Continuous: I'm having my hairdresser cut my hair.
Present Perfect : I have had my hairdresser cut my hair
Present Perfect continuous: I have been having my hairdresser cut my hair.
Simple past: I had my hairdresser cut my hair.
Past Continuous: I was having my hairdresser cut my hair.
Past Perfect: I had had my hairdresser cut my hair.
Past Perfect continuous: I had been having my hairdresser cut my hair.
Simple Future: I will have my hairdresser cut my hair.
Future Continuous: I will be having my hairdresser cut my hair.
Future Perfect Continuous: I will have been having my hairdresser cut my hair.
Going to: I am going to have my hairdresser cut my hair.
Modals: I may/might/etc have my hairdresser cut my hair.

Get someone to do something

Simple Present:	I get the hairdresser to cut my hair.
Present Continuous:	I'm getting the hairdresser to cut my hair.
Present Perfect:	I have gotten my hairdresser to cut my hair.
Present Perfect Continuous:	I have been getting my hairdresser to cut my hair.
Simple Past:	I got my hairdresser to cut my hair.
Past Continuous:	I was getting my hairdresser to cut my hair.
Past Perfect:	I had got my hairdresser to cut my hair.
Past Perfect Continuous:	I had been getting my hairdresser to cut my hair.
Simple Future:	I will get my hairdresser to cut my hair.
Future continuous:	I will be getting my hairdresser to cut my hair.
Future Perfect:	I will have gotten my hairdresser to cut my hair.
Future Perfect Continuous:	I will have been getting my hairdresser to cut my hair.
Going to+Infinitive:	I am going to get my hairdresser to cut my hair.
Modal+Bare Infinitive:	I can/may/might/etc get my hairdresser to cut my hair.

Helen Boubouli **Grammar Genie**

CONDITIONALS

Type 0
For general truths or situations or conditions which are always true:

If+ Simple present, ⇒ Simple Present

If water freezes, it turns into ice.

If I don't eat anything one day, I feel sick.

If I don't sleep, I can't work.

When I study, I do well in tests.

Type 1
True or probable in the Present or Future

If+ Simple Present, present perfect, or present continuous	⇒	will (future)/ simple Present/ can/ may/might/would+ bare infinitive/command (imperative)

 If I see you, I will tell you what happened.

I will tell you what happened If I see you. (without a comma)

If I wake up early**,** I have time to do a lot of things.

I have time to do a lot of things if I wake up early.

If I don't see Nina**,** I won't tell her the news.

If you finish early, you may/ go out and play.

when / if:

If I finish my work, I'll go shopping.(If I don't finish my work, I won't go shopping.)

When I finish my work, I'll go shopping.(I will finish my work first, and then I'll go shopping.)

If you come, we'll serve dinner.(We will only serve dinner if you come. If you don't come, we won't.)

When you come, we'll serve dinner.(We won't serve dinner until you come. We'll wait for you to come, and then we'll serve dinner.)

A comma is used when the time clause or the condition clause comes before the main clause:

If you see Dimitri**,** give him a kiss from me.

Give Dmitri a kiss from me if you see him.

Helen Boubouli   **Gra**m**ar Geni**e

We do not use future (will) after "if" with a future meaning:

Incorrect:**If I will see** Romy, I'll introduce her to you. (**will is not used** in conditionals **with future meaning**)

Correct:If I see Romy, I'll introduce her to you.

We only put a comma when we begin with "if":

If you finish work early**,** you can come with us.

You can come with us if you finish work early.

"Unless" has a negative meaning. That's why the verb that follows is always affirmative (unless=if not):

Unless they invite me, I won't go.(**If they don't invite me,**
 I won't go**.)**

Type 2

Unlikely, imaginary in the Present or Future:

| If+ Simple Past | ⮕ | would
could + bare infinitive
might |

If I saw Nina**, I would tell** her about the test.
(=it is unlikely that I will see Nina)

I would tell Nina about the test **if I saw** her.

If I won a lot of money**, I would travel** around the world.(=I will probably not win a lot of money)

I would travel around the world **if I won** a lot of money. (we use a comma only when we begin the sentence with "if")

We don't use "would" after "if":

Incorrect: **If I would see** Nina, I would tell her about the test.

Correct: If I saw Nina, I would tell her about the test.

Helen Boubouli   **Gram**m**ar Geni**e

*We can use **"were" in all persons,** singular & plural **with the verb "to be"** to express **improbability*** :

If he were/was rich, he would donate a lot of money to charity.

If I were/was you, I would pay attention in class.

You can also **begin the sentence with "were"** instead of "if" followed by the subject. This is called an inversion:

Were I you, I would be grateful.
(=if I were you, ……..)

Were I you, I would not give up so easily.
(=if I were you, ……….)

BUT FOR: If it wasn't for

But for her mum, she wouldn't know how to cook.
(=**if it wasn't for** her mum, she wouldn't know how to cook)

Type 3

Impossible, improbable about the Past:

If + Past Perfect	➲	would + have + past participle could + have + past participle might + have + past participle

If I had seen Romy, **I would have invited** her to dinner.
(=but I didn't see her so I didn't invite her)

I would have gone on the excursion **if I hadn't been** so ill.
(=but I was ill so didn't go)

If we hadn't been so lazy, **we could have done** so many things when we were young.
(=we were too lazy so we didn't do anything)

BUT FOR: If it hadn't been for

But for her husband's support, she would never have succeeded.(=**If it hadn't been for** her husband's support, she would never have succeeded.)

If it hadn't been for your advice, I would probably have made the wrong choices in life.
(=**But for your advice**, I would probably have made the wrong choices in life

Helen Boubouli   **Grammar Genie**

Time and Condition Clauses

Time conjunctions tell us when something happens.

"Will" or "Would" or going to + infinitive are not used after time Conjunctions/clauses.

A comma is used when the time clause or the condition clause comes before the main clause.

As soon as I came home **,** I started packing.

time clause   comma   independent clause

I started packing as soon as I came home

TIME CLAUSES	CONDITION CLAUSES
after as long as as soon as before until	on condition that as long as provided/providing that only if suppose/supposing what if
the moment the minute the next time once until/till (ever) since when whenever while	even if/though if unless in case

After time clauses we use **past tenses to refer to the past, present tenses to refer to the present and future**

Ever since Anna came back from the island, she has been unhappy.

"When"⊃time conjunction
"When"+ present tenses⊃for the present and future

When I see him, I will give him my number

"When + simple past⊃for the past

When I saw him the other day, I gave him my number.

"
"When" after the words **"I don't know",** can be followed by future tenses

I don't know when I will see you again.

Helen Boubouli   **Grammar Genie**

Unreal Past Tenses with "Wish" = "If only"

Wish/if only+ Simple Past	⮕**be sorry about a PRESENT situation**	(Chris isn't here) I wish he was/were.
Wish/if only + Past Continuous	⮕be sorry about a PRESENT situation	I wish I was/were coming. (=I'm not coming)
Wish/if only + Past Perfect	⮕ **be sorry about a PAST situation**	I wish I had gone to the party.(=Why didn't I go?)
Wish/if only + Past Perfect Continuous	⮕ be sorry about a PAST situation	I wish I had been sleeping.(Why wasn't I sleeping?)
Wish/if only + Could/ Would	⮕ **a wish for the FUTURE**	I wish you would come with me. (=Why don't you come with me?)
Wish/if only + Could/ Would	⮕a strong wish for the PRESENT	I wish he would call me. (=Why doesn't he call?)
Wish/if only + Could/ Would	⮕annoyance in the present	I wish you would stop talking. (=Why are you always talking?)
		I wish you wouldn't lie all the time. (=Why are you always lying?)
		I wish you would stop lying

83

INDIRECT SPEECH (REPORTED SPEECH)

Direct speech is giving a person's exact words using (quotation marks):

She said, **"I like learning the English."**

Indirect speech is when we are reporting what someone has said:

She said that she liked learning English.

Introductory verbs most commonly used

Tell someone something, say something, ask, replied. "Tell" is always followed by an object pronoun, (me, you ,him, her, it, us, them,) or proper noun "Evans, Andrew," etc.

She told me that she was coming the following week.

I told Anthony that I wasn't going to lie to his parents.

but

She said that she was coming the following week.

I said that I wasn't going to lie to Anthony's parents.

Helen Boubouli   **Grammar Genie**

Punctuation

Quotation marks (" ") are used to report somebody's exact words or thoughts:

" I work hard"

A comma is placed after said if it's in the beginning.

She said, "I work hard."

" I work hard," she said.

Quotation marks are added after the full stop.

She said, "I work hard."

Personal pronouns

Personal pronouns and possessive adjectives change, accordingly, when reporting someone else's words:

"**I** will not see **you** tomorrow." She said.

She said that **she** would not see **me** the following day.

Tense changes:

When we are reporting someone else's words the **tenses change if the introductory verb is in the simple past.** It is helpful to remember that **we go one tense back into the past** when we change the tenses in indirect speech:

"I **am** happy" ⮕ She **said,** that she **was** happy.
"I **am** happy" ⮕ She **says,** that she **is** happy.(no change)

Direct speech	Indirect speech
She said, "I work hard." "I work hard," she said.	She said(that) she worked hard.
She said, "I am working hard." "I am working hard," she said.	She said (that) she was working hard.
She said, "I have worked hard." "I have worked hard," she said.	She said (that) she had worked hard.
She said, "I have been working hard." "I have been working hard," she said.	She said (that) she had been working hard.

Helen Boubouli   **Gram**m**ar Geni**e

She said, "I worked hard."
"I worked hard," she said.
She said, "I was working hard."
"I was working hard," she said.
She said, "I will work hard."
"I will work hard," she said.
She said, "I will be working hard."
"I will be working hard," she said.
She said,"I may work hard."
"I may work hard," she said.
She said, "I can work hard."
"I can work hard," she said.
She said, "I must/have to work hard."(obligation)
"I must/have to work hard," she said.
She said, "I must not work hard."
She said, "I must be wrong"

She said (that) she had worked hard.

She said (that) she had been working hard.

She said (that) she would work hard.

She said (that) she would be working hard.

She said (that) she might work hard.

She said (that) she could work hard.

She said(that) she had to work hard.

She said (that) she must be wrong.

87

(deduction, assumption) "I must be wrong," she said.	(no change for deduction, assumption)
She said, "I am going to work hard." "I am going to work hard," she said.	She said (that) she was going to work hard.
She said, "I needn't work hard." "I needn't work hard," she said.	She said (that) she didn't need to work hard.
She said, "I didn't need to work hard." "I didn'tneed to work hard," she said.	She said (that) she hadn't needed to work to work hard.
would, could, might, should, used to, ought to and had to, must (assumption, deduction)	No change

All the words of time and place change if the introductory verb is in the simple past:

She said, "I'm coming back home next year."

She said (that) she was coming back home the following year.

Changes of words of time and place:

Direct speech	Indirect speech
today/ tonight/ this week/month/year	that day, that night, that week/month/year
yesterday	the day before/the previous day
last week/month/year	the week/month/year before/the previous week/month/year
a wee /month/year ago	the week/month/year before/the previous week/month/year
tomorrow	the day after/the next day/the following day
next week/month/year	the following week/month/year the next week/month/year
here	there

"I **will give** you an answer **next week**," he said.

He said(that) he **would give** me an answer **the following week.**

" George **told me** the truth **yesterday**," he said.

He said,(that) George **had told him** the truth **the day before.**

A number of other word changes:

Direct speech	Indirect speech
this	**that**
these	**those**
here	**there**
come	**go**
now	**then**

He said, "**This is** the house I like."

He said **that was** the house he liked.

She said, "I want to **come** with you to London."

She said she wanted **to go** with me to London.

No changes are made in indirect speech if or when the introductory **verb is in simple present, present perfect or simple future:**

She says, "**I'm coming** back home next year."

She **says** (that) **she is coming** back home next year."

we are reporting a general truth:

He said, "**The sun revolves** around the earth."

He said (that) **the sun revolves** around the earth.

we are reporting a permanent state:

She said**, "I live** in London."

She said that **she lives** in London.

we have 2nd or 3rd conditional even if the introductory verb is in simple past:

"If you had talked to me, I would have helped you." she said.

She said (that) if I had talked to her, she would have helped me.

"If I were you, I would not marry him." She said.

She said that if she were me, she would not marry him.

we have unreal past:

She said, "It's time you answered some questions."

She said (that) it was time I answered some questions.

She said, "I would rather you had not come."

She said (that) she would rather we/ I had not come.

The children said, "We wish we didn't have school today."

The children said (that) they wish they didn't have school today.

we have past perfect or past perfect continuous:

He said, "I had been working."

He said (that) he had been working.

we are reporting somebody's words right after they are said:

The teacher told Irene, "You are cheating on the test."

The teacher told Irene that she is cheating on the test.

we have **would, could, might, should, used to, ought to and had to, must (assumption, deduction)** in the sentence:

He said, "We should leave immediately"

He said (that) they should leave immediately.

He said, "I could try to help you."

He said, (that) she could try to help us.

He said, "Veronica must be sick."**(assumption)**

He said that Veronica must be sick.

but

"You **must inform** every one of the changes." He said. **(obligation)**

He said that **I had to inform** every one of the changes.

Indirect Questions (reported questions)

When reporting interrogative sentences (questions) it is important to remember that **the sentences become affirmative:**

Direct speech	Indirect speech
"What are you doing?"	**She asked me what I was doing.**
"Where are you going?"	**She asked me where I was going.**
"Why did you do that?"	**She asked me why I had done that.**
"What is your name?"	**She asked me what my name is/was.**

Wrong	Correct
❌ She asked me what was I doing?	✅ **She asked me what I was doing.**
❌ She asked me where was I going?	✅ **She asked me where I was going.**
❌ She asked me why had I done that?	✅ **She asked me why I had done that.**
❌ She asked me what was my name?	✅ **She asked me what my name is /was.**

"We use if/whether to report yes/no questions.
"Whether" is usually more formal and is used when there is a choice between two things:

Direct speech	Indirect speech
"Did you rest?"	**He asked me if/whether I had rested.**

When we are reporting sentences with a time word such as **who, why, when, where, etc.** we use the same time word:

Direct speech	**Indirect speech**
"Where did you go last night?"	**He asked me where I had gone the previous night.**
"Why are you late?"	**He asked me why I was late.**
"When is she coming?"	**He asked me when she was coming.**
"Where do they live?"	**He asked me where they live.**
"Who has she been meeting?"	**He asked me who she had been meeting.**

Introductory verbs used when reporting interrogative sentences: **ask/want to know/wonder/inquire,etc.**

Reporting the imperative (orders, requests, suggestions)

POSITIVE IMPERATIVE⮕tell/order/advise/ask etc+person+full infinitive

Direct speech:	Indirect speech
"Leave the room."	He told me to leave the room.

NEGATIVE IMPERATIVE⮕tell/ order/advice/ask etc + person + (not) +full infinitive.

Direct speech	Indirect speech
"Don't tell them"	He told me not to tell them.
"You should not leave ."	He advised me not to leave.
"Could you please not tell anybody."	He asked me not to tell anybody.

Verb+object+ full infinitive

advise	"You should talk to a lawyer."	She **advised me to talk to** a lawyer.
ask	"Could you please help me lift this box."	**She asked Gus to help her lift that box.**
allow	"You can go out and play."	She **allowed us to go** out and play.
beg	"Please keep this a secret."	She **begged me to keep** that a secret.
forbid	"Kids, you are forbidden to go outside."	He **forbade us to go** outside.
invite	"Would you like to come to my party."	He **invited me (to go)to** his party.
instruct	"Make sure you read the label before you wash it."	He **instructed me to first read** the label before I washed it.
order	"Leave at this moment."	She **ordered us to leave.**
permit	"You can smoke outside."	She **permitted us to smoke** outside.
remind	"Don't forget to set the alarm."	She **reminded her to set** the alarm.

More introductory verbs:

Other introductory verbs used to report what someone said without using the exact words they said:

Verb+ object pronoun/proper noun(sb) +full infinitive

want	"I would like you to trust me."	**He** wanted me to trust **him.**
warn	"You'll catch a cold if you go outside without your coat on."	She **warned me not to go** outside without my coat on.

Verb+ full infinitive

agree	"Yes, I'll come with you."	She agreed to come with me.
decide	"I'll stay home and relax today."	She decided to stay home and relax that day.
demand	"I have to see you now."	He demanded to see me now.
offer	"I'll help you clean up."	He offered to help me clean up.
promise	"I'll take you to the cinema tomorrow."	He promised to take me to the cinema the following day.
prefer	"I would rather stay home."	He prefers to stay home
refuse	"No, I won't help you."	He refused to help me.
threaten	"I will punish you if you go out, kids"	He threatened to punish us if we went out.
volunteer	"I'll babysit tonight, so you can go out."	She volunteered/ offered to babysit that night so that we could go out.

Helen Boubouli **Gramm**a**r Geni**e

verb+ that clause

	"I stole your USB."	He admitted that he had stolen my USB.
admit		
agree	"Why not, I'll come with you."	**He agreed that** he would come with me.
announce	"We're getting married the 15th of August."	**They announced that** they were getting married the 15th of August.
boast	"No one is more experienced than me."	**He boasted that** no one was more experienced than him.
claim	"I am an actor."	**He claimed that** he was an actor
complain	"You always go to work late."	**He complained that** I always went to work late."
decide	"I made up my mind. I'm going to Spain on my vacation."	**He decided that** he was going to Spain on his vacation.
deny	"I never cheated in an exam."	**He denied that** he had ever cheated in an exam.
exclaim	"You won!" "What a	He exclaimed that I had won.

	beautiful day!"	He exclaimed that it was a beautiful day. He exclaimed what a beautiful day it was.
explain	"You have to beat the eggs before putting them in the pan."	He explained that I had to beat the eggs before putting them in the pan.
insist	He should be informed immediately	I insist that he be informed immediately
recommend	"You should try that new Chinese restaurant."	He recommended that I try that new Chinese restaurant.
report	"Several people have been arrested"	It was reported that several people had been arrested.
suggest	"You should be more quiet."	He suggested that I (should) be more quiet. "He should see a doctor."
threaten	"If you don't study "I will have to talk to your parents."	He threatened that he would talk to my parents if I didn't study.

Helen Boubouli **Gramm**a**r Geni**e

verb+gerund
verb+preposition+gerund

apologise for	"I'm sorry for lying to you."	**He apologised for lying** to me.
boast about	"I'm the smartest."	**He boasted about being** the smartest.
insist on	'They still play their music after midnight even though the neighbours are complaining.	**They insist on playing** their music after midnight.
complain about	"I'm always working late."	**He's always complaining about working** late.

Verb+ object(sb)+preposition+gerund

accuse someone of	"He lied to me."	**She accused him of lying** to her.
congratulate someone on	"Congratulations! You passed the proficiency exam."	**He congratulated me on passing** the proficiency exam.
complain to somebody about	"I'm always working late."	**He's always complaining to me about working** late.

Helen Boubouli   **Grammar Genie**

QUESTION TAGS

Question tags are **small questions at the end of a sentence** used to **ask for confirmation to affirmative and negative sentences.** They are formed, the same way we form questions, with an **auxiliary verb +subject pronoun:**

You are English, **aren't you?**

You are not English**, are you?**

Positive statement➲ negative question tag
Negative statement➲positive question tag

You **are** sick, **aren't you?**

You **are not** sick**, are you?**

You **can** tell me, **can't you?**

You don't like me**, do you?**

If there is an auxiliary verb in the sentence, we use that auxiliary verb to form a question tag:

You **are** sick, **aren't you?**

He **will** come, **won't** he?

He **has left, hasn't he?**

If there is no auxiliary verb in the sentence, we use **do/does for simple present** and **did for simple past:**

You **work** hard, **don't you?**

You **don't work** hard, **do you?**

You **told** him, **didn't** you?

You **didn't tell** him, **did** you?

Everyone/everybody/someone/somebody/anyone/anybody/no one/nobody/these/those take "they" in the tag:

Everyone came, **didn't they?**

Someone has told her**, haven't they?**

Anybody could have told him, **couldn't they?**

Those are mine, **aren't they?**

Nothing/this/that take **it** in the tag:

This is absurd, **isn't it?**

That's finished, **isn't it?**

Nothing was done about it, **was it?**

Helen Boubouli   **Grammar Genie**

Hardly (ever), no(one), nothing, nobody, nowhere, neither, never, rarely, seldom, scarcely, are negative words which take an **affirmative tag:**

Nobody came, **did they?**

Hardly anyone came, **did they?**

Never forget this, **will you?**

Nothing was done heard, **was it?**

She can **hardly** talk, **can she?**

When we have **there** in a sentence, we can also use **"there" in the question tag:**

There is nothing to talk about, **is there?**

There was a misunderstanding, **wasn't there?**

Special Question Tags:

1) "I am"	**"aren't I?"**	I am late, **aren't** I? ➲**informal** I am late, **am I not?** ➲ formal
2) "Let's"	**"shall we?"**	Let's begin, **shall we?**
3) "Let me/her" etc	**"will you?"**	Let me help you, **will you/ won't you?**
4) Imperative (orders/requests)	**"will /won't/ can/can't/ would you?"**	Open the window, **will you/won't you/can you/ can't you/would you?** ➲**imperative** Tell me, **will you/can you?** ➲**friendly request** Tell me, **won't you/can't you?** (This is a friendly request. The speaker is quite annoyed, though.)
5) "Don't (negative imperative)	**"will you?"**	Don't leave, **will you?** ➲**negative imperative**
6) Polite suggestions/offers/ invitations	**"won't you?"**	Have a drink, **won't you?** ➲**polite offer** Consult a lawyer, **won't you?** ➲**polite suggestion**
7) "This is/That is"	**"isn't it?"**	**This is final, isn't it?**
8) "I have" (possession)	**"haven't I?"**	He has three kids, **hasn't he?** ➲**possession**
9) "I have" (Idiom) "I had"	**"don't I?"** **"didn't I"**	They had a nice time, **didn't they**➲**idiom**
10) "I used to"	**"didn't I?"**	They used to be friends, **didn't they?**

106

Helen Boubouli   **Grammar Genie**

everybody/everyone/anybody	
anybody/anyone	
nobody/no one	➲ **become "they"**
neither	**in question tags**
none	
these/those	

Everybody is sick today, **aren't they?**

Nobody knows what happened**, do they?**

Those books are mine**, aren't they?**

everybody/everyone/anybody	
anybody/anyone	
nobody/no one	➲ **used with**
neither	**singular verbs**
none	
these/those	

Everybody **believes** what you are saying. **don't they?**

Someone **is** absent, **aren't they?**

Nobody **likes** what you are doing, **do they?**

Agreement to affirmative sentences
So +auxiliary +subject
or
Subject +auxiliary +too

I like sports	**So does he**	He does too
He is studying	**So is she**	She is too
We missed the bus	**So did they**	They did too
I have finished	**So have we**	We have too
They had seen him	**So had we**	We had too
He will come	**So will they**	They will too

Agreement to negative sentences
(neither/nor +auxiliary +subject)
or
(subject +auxiliary +not +either)

I don't like football	**Neither/nor does she**	She doesn't either
He is not studying	**Neither/nor is she**	She isn't either
We didn't miss the bus	**Neither/nor did they**	They didn't either
I haven't finished yet	**Neither/nor have we**	We haven't either
They hadn't seen him	**Neither/nor had we**	We hadn't either
They won't see him	**Neither will we**	We won't either

Disagreement to affirmative sentences
(But+)subject pronoun/noun +negative auxiliary verb

I like football	He doesn't	**(I like football,** but he doesn't)
John is studying	**Ann isn't**	(John is studying, **but Ann isn't)**
We missed the bus.	**They didn't**	(We missed the bus, **but they didn't.)**
I have finished	**We haven't**	(I have finished, **but we haven't)**
They had seen him	**We hadn't**	(They had seen him, **but we hadn't)**
He will come	**We will not**	(He will come, **but we will not)**

Disagreement to negative sentences

(But+)subject pronoun/noun +affirmative auxiliary verb

I don't like football	He does	**(I don't like sports,** but he does)
Tim is not studying	**Helen is**	(Tim is not studying, **but Helen is)**
We didn't miss the bus	**They did**	(We didn't miss the bus, **but they did)**

I haven't finished yet	**They have**	(I haven't finished yet, **but they have**)
They hadn't seen him	**We had**	(They hadn't seen him, **but we had**)
He will not come	**We will**	(He will not come, **but we will**)

So/not:

Using **so** and **not** in answers after the following verbs:**think, believe, expect, suppose**, **imagine, hope, seem, be afraid, appear, tell somebody.**

Affirmative answers	Negative answers 1
I think so	**I don't think so**
I believe so	**I don't believe so**
I expect so	**I don't expect so**
I suppose so	**I don't suppose so**
I imagine so	**I don't imagine so**
It seems so	**It doesn't seem so**

I'm afraid so	------------- -------------
I guess so	------------- ------------- -
I hope so	------------- ------------- -

-Will you be coming to see us today?
-I think so. I have the day off.

-Is it going to be sunny this morning?
-It seems so. The sun is out already.

-Is Ann going to take part in the contest?
-She told me so. I hope she doesn't change her mind.

-Do you like our new neighbours?
-I guess so. They seem nice.

-Will you be moving to your new house soon?
-I don't imagine so. It still needs a lot of doing up.

ADJECTIVES/ADVERBS

Use:
An adjective describes or modifies a noun or a pronoun or comes after certain verbs, **be, feel, look, seem, sound, smell, taste etc.** to describe how something is:

He is a **fast** driver.
He is a **careful** driver.
He looks **tired**.
I feel **exhausted**.
Jim is a **diligent** student.
Helen is a **smart** girl.
I feel **optimistic** about the outcome of the elections.
The stew tastes **delicious**.

There are adjectives that end in – **ed** and adjectives ending in – **ing**

Adjectives used to talk about **how somebody feels** end in **-ed**: **bored, interested, disappointed, excited, surprised:**

I am interested **in reading science fiction books.**
I'm so **bored today.**

Helen Boubouli   **Grammar Geni**e

Adjectives used to talk about how **something has influenced somebody** end in **-ing:** **boring, interesting, disappointing, exciting, surprising:**

I find science fiction books interesting.
What a boring day **this is!**

Adjectives have no plural form and no gender:

| a **beautiful** girl | **beautiful** girls |
| a **good-looking** man | **good-looking** men |

Nouns can also be used as adjectives. **When nouns are used as adjectives they are always singular:**

☑ **cat food**	☒ **cats food**
☑ **apple juice**	☒ **apples** juice
☑ **a five-day trip**	☒ a five-**days** trip
☑ **a ten-year-old boy**	☒ a ten-**years**-old boy
☑ **a four-week vacation**	☒ a four-**weeks** vacation

It is not unusual in English to use more than one adjective before a noun. **The correct order of adjectives in a sentence is the following:**

opinion +size+ age+ shape + color+origin(nationality)+ material +purpose +noun

A bright tall thirty–year old thin Greek woman

A big one-family country house

Structure:

Adjectives that end in **-e** form their adverbs by adding **-ly** to the ending.

Adjective	**Adverb**
rare	rarely

Adjectives that end in **-le** preceded by a consonant form their adverbs by **dropping the- le and adding- ly.**

Adjective	**Adverb**
simple	simply
favorable	favorably

Helen Boubouli   **Grammar Geni**e

Adjectives that end in **-le** preceded by a vowel form their adverbs by **just adding-ly to the adjective.**

Adjective   **Adverb**
sole   solely

EXCEPTION: In the case of **"whole"** the final "e" is removed before adding the "ly".

whole   **wholly**

Adverbs answer the questions, where**? when? how? why?** and **to what extent?**
An adverb describes or modifies a verb, an adjective or another adverb:

He drives fast.

He drives very carefully.

He waited patiently **for the results to come out.**

The well-recited poem **left everyone speechless.**

Everyone was at a loss for words at the wonderfully-performed play.

Unfortunately, **we did not arrive in time for the Christmas feast yesterday.**

Some words that **end in-ly** are used both as adjectives and adverbs:**daily, weekly, yearly, monthly, lonely, ugly, awful, friendly:**

We have weekly **teachers' meetings.(adjective)**

We meet weekly to talk about our students.(adverb)

She's an awful **person. (adjective)**

She talks awful.**(adverb)**

Adjectives that **end in –ly** should not be confused with adverbs:

Maria has **weekly** sessions with her shrink. (adjective)

Maria sees her shrink **weekly.**(adverb)

Helen Boubouli **Grammar Genie**

Some irregular adverbs have the same adjective form:

Adjective	Adverb
fast	fast
hard	hard
early	early
awful	awful
late	late
high	high
low	low
near	near
deep	deep
wide	wide
lovely	lovely

Adjective	Adverb
He is an **awful person**.	The kids are behaving **awful** today.
He is a **fast driver**.	He drives **fast**.
He has high grades.	He climbed **high**.
She has low grades.	He stooped really **low**.
He's a **hard worker**.	He works **hard**.
I'm **near-sighted**.	I live **near** the subway.

We distinguish adjectives from adverbs that have the same form by identifying what they describe.

An adjective describes a noun where **as an adverb describes a verb:**

> I had a **hard** day.(**adjective**)

> I work **hard**.(**adverb**)

When **fast, hard, early, late, low, high, awful, wide, deep, near** take the suffix **–ly** to form their adverbs, their meaning is different than that of their adjectives:

Deeply (extremely)	I'm **deeply touched.**
Hardly (almost never)	I **hardly** ever see you any more.
Widely (to a large extent)	A controversial topic is something **widely** discussed.
Lately (recently)	Have you seen any good films **lately?**
Nearly (almost)	We've been living here for **nearly** ten years.
Awfully(very)	I am **awfully** tired.
Highly(very)	It is **highly** unlikely that he'll show up for dinner.
	He's **highly regarded/ esteemed** for his ethics. (respected)

Helen Boubouli   **Grammar Genie**

> We use **"bad" with state verbs** and **"badly" with action verbs.** However some **verbs that describe feelings can be both action verbs and state verbs.** You have to know the meaning that the specific verb wants to convey.

We use the adjective "bad" to describe emotions, feelings and states **and the adverb** "badly" to descrive actions:

I feel **bad**
You are **bad**
The kids are behaving **badly**
The dog smells **badly**(=he doesn't have the ability to smell using his nose)
The dog smells **bad**(=he needs a bath)
I need to see you **badly**(=very much)

THE COMPARATIVE AND SUPERLATIVE OF ADJECTIVES

We use the comparative to compare two people or things and the superlative to compare two or more people or things.

To form the comparative and the superlative of one-syllable adjectives (short adjectives) with more than 1 vowel or more than 1 consonant at the end of the word we use **-er for the comparative and -est for the superlative:**

Adjective	Comparative	Superlative
old	older	oldest
fast	faster	fastest
new	newer	newest
short	shorter	shortest
smart	smarter	smartest

You're **much older than I thought** you were.

She's **the oldest athlete in the team.**

For one syllable adjectives ending in -e we add -r to the adjective to form the comparative and -est to form the superlative:

Adjective	Comparative	Superlative
nice	nicer	nicest

Helen Boubouli   **Grammar Genie**

For one syllable adjectives with 1 vowel and 1 consonant at the end of the word we double the consonant and add **-er** to form the comparative and **-est** to form the superlative:

Adjective	Comparative	Superlative
big	bigger	biggest
fat	fatter	fattest
sad	sadder	saddest
hot	hotter	hottest

For two-syllable adjectives ending in y we change the y to an i and add er to the adjective to form the comparative and est to form the superlative :

Adjective	Comparative	Superlative
sunny	sunnier	sunniest
happy	happier	happiest
pretty	prettier	prettiest

For two or more syllable adjectives (longer adjectives) that do not end in y we add more or less before the adjective to form the comparative and the most or the least for the superlative:

Adjective	Comparative	Superlative
beautiful	**more beautiful**	the most beautiful
interesting	**more interesting**	the most interesting
bored	**more bored**	the most bored
boring	**more boring**	the most boring
excited	**more excited**	most excited

For some two or more syllable adjectives (longer adjectives) that do not end in y we add er before the adjective to form the comparative and est for the superlative:

Adjective	Comparative	Superlative
clever	clever**er**	clever**est**
quick	quick**er**	quick**est**

Adjectives that are **hyphenated (compound adjectives)** form their **comparative with more and superlative with most**:
Nick is **more hard-working than John**.

Nick is **the most hard-working boy** in the class.

Helen Boubouli   **Grammar Genie**

Adjectives that have irregular comparative and superlative forms:

Adjective	Comparative	Superlative
good	better	best
bad	worse	worst
far	farther	farthest
far	further	furthest
little	less	least
much	more	most
many	more	most

This is **the best performance I have ever seen.**

You're **better at Maths than me.**

People nowadays have **less money** for consumption **than they used to** 20 years ago.

I know that I'm giving **the least of all** towards charity.

Expressions used in the superlative:**in the world, of them all, I have ever seen/been to, etc**.

Vatican City is the **smallest country in the world.**

Los Angeles is one of the **nicest places I have ever been to.**

Grammar Genie

Two-Syllable Adjectives that can be used both with **-er** and **-est** and with **more** and **most**:

Two-Syllable Adjective	Comparative Form	Superlative Form
clever	cleverer/ more clever	cleverest /most clever
friendly	friendlier/ more friendly	friendliest/ most friendly
funny	funnier/ more funny	funniest/ most funny
gentle	gentler /more gentle	gentlest/ most gentle
quiet	quieter/ more quiet	quietest/ most quiet
simple	simpler /more simple	simplest /most simple

The kids in my English class are **friendlier than/more friendly than** the kids in my Math class.

The kids in my English class are **the friendliest/ the most friendly** in the whole school.

THE COMPARATIVE AND SUPERLATIVE OF ADVERBS

Adverbs answer the questions, **where? when? how? Why? and to "what extent?"**
An adverb describes or modifies a verb, an adjective or another adverb :

He drives **fast**.
He drives very **carefully**.
He waited **patiently** for the results to come out.
Everyone was at a loss for words at the **wonderfully-performed** play.
Unfortunately, we did not arrive in time for the Christmas feast yesterday.

One syllable adverbs take **er** to form the comparative and **est** to form the superlative:

Adverb	Comparative	Superlative
hard	**harder**	**hardest**
fast	**faster**	**fastest?**

Helen Boubouli   **Gramm**ar Geni**e**

One or two syllable adverbs ending in ly become lier to form the comparative and liest to form the superlative:

Adverb	Comparative	Superlative
lovely	**lovelier**	**loveliest**
early	**earlier**	**earliest**
quickly	**quicklier**	**quickliest**

For adverbs formed by adding the suffix ly to the adjectives we form the comparative with more or less and the superlative with most or least:

Adjective	Adverb	Comparative Adverb	Superlative Adverb
slow	slowly	more slowly	most slowly
happy	happily	more happily	most happily
quiet	quietly	more quietly	most quietly
careful	carefully	more carefully	most carefully

For two or more syllable adverbs we use more or less before the adverb to form the comparative and most or least to form the superlative:

Adjective	Adverb	Comparative Adverb	Superlative Adverb
interesting	interestingly	more interestingly	most interestingly
beautiful	beautifully	more beautifully	most beautifully

Irregular adverbs:

Some irregular adverbs that have the same adjective form take the suffix er to form the comparative and est to form the superlative:

Adjective	Adverb	Comparative Adverb	Superlative Adverb
fast	fast	faster	fastest
hard	hard	harder	hardest
early	early	earlier	earliest
late	late	later	latest
high	high	higher	highest
low	low	lower	lowest
near	near	nearer	nearest
deep	deep	deeper	deepest
wide	wide	wider	widest
lovely	lovely	lovelier	loveliest

The following adverbs, **hardly, nearly, lately, deeply, widely,** have a different meaning than their adjectives:

Nearly=	**almost**
Hardly=	**very rarely, very little**
Lately=	**recently**
Deeply=	**very**
Widely=	**by a lot of people**

I **hardly** know him(=I know him very little.)

Helen Boubouli   **Gramm**a**r Geni**e

I'm so busy with work and all that I **hardly** go out any more. (=I very rarely go out.)

I haven't seen him **lately.** I don't know what he's up to.(=I haven't seen him recently.)

I **nearly** fell and broke my leg.(=I almost fell and broke my leg.)

More comparisons:
Not as/so/+ adjective/adverb+ as⮕in negative sentences

Anthony doesn't work **as/so/ hard as** Jim.

By far the + superlative

She is **by far** the best student.

Much(far) + comparative adjective

You're **much smarter** than you think.

You're **far better** than me.

Many more + plural countable noun

I've been to **many more** places than you have.

Much more (+uncountable noun)

I know **much more** than you do.

I have **much more** experience in this job than you.

Agreement to affirmative sentences So +auxiliary +subject *or* Subject +auxiliary +too		
I like sports	**So does he**	**He does too**
He is studying	**So is she**	**She is too**
We missed the bus	**So did they**	**They did too**
I have finished	**So have we**	**We have too**
They had seen him	**So had we**	**We had too**
He will come	**So will they**	**They will too**

Agreement to negative sentences
(Neither/nor +auxiliary +subject)
or
(Subject +auxiliary +not +either)

I don't like football	**Neither/nor does she**	**She doesn't either**
He is not studying	**Neither/nor is she**	**She isn't either**
We didn't miss the bus	**Neither/nor did they**	**They didn't either**
I haven't finished yet	**Neither/nor have we**	**We haven't either**
They hadn't seen him	**Neither/nor had we**	**We hadn't either**
They won't see him	**Neither will we**	**We won't either**

Clauses of result

So-Such

Result clauses, introduced by conjunctions of result, are used to show the result of an action or a situation.

so+ adjective/adverb +that+ full sentence

It was **so** cold that I couldn't go out.

Such+ a/an+adjective+singular countable noun(+ full sentence)

It was **such a cold day** that I couldn't go out.

It was **such a lovely day** that we decided to go for a picnic.

Such +adjective+uncountable noun/plural noun(+ full sentence)

*It was **such nice weather** that we decided to go on a picnic.

They are **such nice people** that you really should meet them.

*There's no article before "weather" as "weather" is uncountable.
An article is not used before uncountable nouns and plural nouns.

Such+a lot of+uncountable noun/plural countable noun(+ full sentence)

I have **such a lot of** money that I don't need to work.

Such a lot of people attended the concert that the stadium was packed.

so few/ many+plural countable noun+(that)+ full sentence

I have **so many** friends that I always have someone to turn to.

So little/ much/+uncountable noun+(that)+ full sentence

I have **so little** time that I have to ask you to leave.

He has **so much** money that he's giving away some to charity

Too/enough

too/enough+adjective:

Too+ adjective+ (for me/him/her/ you etc.) to do something

It was **too cold** for **me to go** out.

Adjective+ enough + to do something

It **wasn't warm enough** (for me) **to go** out.

(much) (far) too+adjective:

(much) (far) too+ adjective

It was **(much) (far) too cold**(for me) **to go** out.

(=it was very cold, so I couldn't go out)

The chilly is(**much) too spicy to eat.**

(=it was very spicy, so I couldn't eat it)

but

(much)(far) too much + uncountable noun

You put **(much) too much pepper** in the chilly.

(=you put a lot of pepper in the chilly)

134

Helen Boubouli **Grammar Genie**

(much)(far) too many + plural noun

There are **too many people** in this room,

(=There are a lot of people in this room)

There are **much too many students** in this room.

You asked **far too many questions.**

adjective + enough (for me/him/her/you/Ann etc)

The weather is not **warm enough to go** swimming.

Tim is not **old enough to go** out without an escort.

Clauses of concession or contrast clauses

although/even though/though +clause(subject+verb)

Although/Even though I'm wealthy, I refuse to waste my money.

I refuse to waste my money **even though** I'm wealthy.

Note: we can also put though at the end of the sentence

I'm wealthy. I refuse to waste my money **though.**

Despite/In spite of +noun or gerund
In spite of the fact that +clause(subject+verb)
Despite the fact that+clause(subject+verb)

Despite being wealthy, I refuse to waste my money.

I refuse to waste my money **despite** being wealthy.

I refuse to waste my money **despite the fact that** I'm wealthy.

nevertheless
nonetheless
however...(still)

> **We always use a comma after: However, Nonetheless, Nevertheless**

I'm quite rich; **nevertheless,** I refuse to waste my money.

I'm quite rich; **nonetheless,** I refuse to waste my money.

I'm quite rich; **however,** I refuse to waste my money.

> **If the conjunction is in the middle of the sentence, we use two commas:**

I'm quite rich. I refuse**, however,** to waste my money.

but...still

yet...(still)

still

(and)yet

I'm quite rich**,** **but** I refuse to waste my money.

I'm quite rich, **but I still** refuse to waste my money.

I'm quite rich, **(and) yet** I refuse to waste my money.

I'm quite rich, **but** I refuse to waste my money anyway.

He studies little, **yet** he does well in school.

He writes very fast, **yet** legibly.

He's quite rich ,**yet** unwilling to spend money.

but
while+clause
where(as)

While I might be rich, I refuse to spend my money on useless things.

I am self confident, **where(as)** /**while** he is very shy.

I am rich**, but** I refuse to spend my money on useless things.

on the one hand(used at the beginning of the first sentence)

on the other hand(used at the beginning of the second sentence)

(Even) though/Although it was raining, we went out.

It was raining. We went out **though.**

Despite the rain, we went out.

In spite of the rain, we went out

We went out **in spite of** the rain.

We went out **in spite of the fact that** it was raining.

It was raining. **Nevertheless,** we went out.

It was raining; **nonetheless,** we went out.

It was raining. **However**, we went out.

It was raining. **However,** we (**still**) went out

It was raining, **but** we went out.

It was raining, **but we still** went out.

It was raining, **but** we went out **anyway.**

It was raining, **yet** we **still** went out.

It was raining. **Still** we went out.

I'm learning English, **but** Helen is learning Chinese

I'm learning Chinese, **where as** Helen is not.

I'm learning English, **while** Helen is learning Chinese.

I'm learning English, **where (as)** Helen is learning Chinese.

Where (as) Helen is learning Chinese, I'm learning English.

While Helen is learning Chinese, I'm learning English

I'm learning English**; however**, Helen is learning Chinese.

I'm learning English; Helen is learning Chinese, **however.**

I'm learning English; Helen, **on the other hand**, is learning Chinese.

Helen Boubouli   Grammar Genie

THE DEFINITE ARTICLE (THE)

The Definite Article is used with both singular and plural countable and uncountable nouns:

• to refer to something specific.☞	• **The girls are playing in the yard.**
• to refer to a group (type of animal, musical instrument, machine, etc.)☞	• **The tiger** is becoming extinct. • He plays both **the piano** and **the guitar**. • **The typewriter** has become obsolete.

• with various adjectives used as nouns (the young, the elderly, the poor, the rich, etc.) ☞	• The elderly **need affection**. • The poor **should be provided for by the state**.
• before titles (the King, the President, etc.) ☞	• **The headmaster** reprimanded the students. • **The president** of the company has resigned.
• before the names of newspapers (The London Times, the New York Times, The International Herald Tribune, etc.)☞ **Exceptions: foreign newspapers: Le Figaro, Athens News, etc.**	•**The New York Times** is an American daily newspaper. • **The international Herald Tribune** is the Global edition of the New York Times.

141

• **before surnames** (the Smiths, the Bushes, the Jacksons, etc.)☞	• **The Johnsons** moved house.
• **to talk about nationalities when referring to groups of people** (the Spanish, the British, etc.)☞	• **The British** are fairly punctual.

•**to talk about languages** (the Greek language, the French language etc.)	• The English language **is widely spoken.** **also** (=English **is widely spoken.**) • The French language **used to be more popular.** **also** (= French **used to be more popular.**)
• **before rivers** (The Thames, The Mississippi, The Volga.)☞	• **The Volga** is the largest river in Europe.
• **before mountain ranges** (The Himalayas, The Alps, The Pyrenees, etc.) ☞	**The Alps are the highest mountain range in Europe.**
• **before seas or oceans** (the Mediterranean Sea, the Pacific Ocean, the Caribbean Sea, etc.) ☞	• **The Atlantic Ocean** is the second-largest of the world's oceanic divisions.

142

• **before groups of islands** (the Virgin Islands, the Canary islands **etc.**) ☞	• **The US Virgin Islands** is a vacation paradise.
• **with the superlative** (the best, the smartest, the most, the worst, **etc.**) ☞	• This is **the most delicious meal** I have ever had.

• **before objects that are regarded as unique** (the Eiffel Tower, The Parthenon, The Colosseum, the Tower of Pisa, the Sun, the Moon, the Stars, the Sea, the Earth, etc.**)**	•The Parthenon **is the most important surviving building of Classical Greece.**
Exceptions: Big Ben	**Big Ben is** the nick name for the Great Bell of the clock in London.

The definite article is not used:

• when we are not talking about something specific. ☞	• I bought a house.
• to refer to something in general with uncountable or plural nouns.☞	• **English** is an international language. also (=The English language........) • **Physics** is my favourite subject in school. • **Teenagers** are known to rebel.
• before abstract nouns (love, beauty, peace, etc.) ☞	**Peace** is when people are able to resolve their conflicts without violence. **Beauty** is in the eye of the beholder
• before lakes(Lake Michigan, Lake Wanapitei, etc.)☞	•**Lake Michigan** is the largest lake in the United States.
• before continents(Asia, Africa, Europe, etc.) ☞	•**Europe** is one of the worlds seven continents.

Helen Boubouli   **Gram**m**ar Gen**ie

• **before countries or cities** (Greece, France, Italy, Paris, Athens, New york,etc.)☞	•**Athens is the capital and largest city of Greece.**
• **before names** (James Brown, Mr Smith, etc.)☞	**Rowan Atkinson** is the name of the guy who played **Mr Bean.**
• **before meals** (breakfast, lunch, supper, dinner)**when we are talking about a meal in general.** ☞	•I really like having breakfast. (=I like having breakfast in general.) but •I really like the breakfast that they serve in some good hotels.
• **before streets**☞	• I live **on 218 Dewey street.** • I bumped into a friend of mine **on Main street.**
•**before single islands**(Myconos, Santorini, etc.)☞	Myconos is one of the most popular and glamourous Greek isles, well own for its non-stop party atmosphere.
• **before God**☞	**God** is the creator of the universe.

THE INDEFINITE ARTICLE (A/AN)

The Indefinite article is used with singular countable nouns:to talk about something in general: ☞	A boy
To talk about somebody we don't know:☞	**A Mr. Erickson** came to see you earlier.
In measurements: ☞	He earns $3.00 **an/per hour.** He works 30 hours **a/per week.**
To refer to a person's profession: ☞	My niece is **a dentist.** One of my daughters is **a lawyer** and the other one is **an artist**.
Before an adjective or adverb to describe a countable noun:	I had **an awful day.** You are **a very considerate person.**

Helen Boubouli   **Grammar Genie**

The indefinite article **a/an is not used before uncountable nouns.**

Some, any, much, no, a lot of, etc, is possible with uncountable nouns:

☒ What a terrible weather.

☑ What terrible weather.

☒ I would like an advice.

☑ I would like some advice.

☒ I have a very important work to do.

☑ I have very important work to do.

☒ A knowledge of the use of the computer is necessary for this position.

☑ (Some)Knowledge of the use of the computer is necessary for this position.

COUNTABLE NOUNS

boy- boys

Countable nouns are both singular and plural:

They can be used with **a/an** in front of them or a number:	**a** house -two houses
Some can be used in front of countable nouns **to form their plural** form:	a house - **some** houses
The plural of most countable nouns is formed by adding an-**s** to the ending of the singular noun:	table- table**s** bag -bag**s** car- car**s**
The plural of nouns ending in-**s**, -**ss**, -**sh**, -**ch**, and -**x** is formed by adding –**es**:	chur**ch** - church**es** bru**sh**- brush**es**
The plural of most nouns ending in –"**o**" is formed by adding-"**es**":	her**o**-hero**es** mang**o**- mang**oes** mosquit**o**- mosquit**oes** potat**o**- potat**oes** tomat**o**- tomat**oes** tornad**o**- tornad**oes** volcan**o**- volcan**oes**
If the words ending in –"**o**" derive from other languages an –"**s**" is added to form their plural:	banj**o**-banj**os** concert**o**- concert**os** phot**o** – phot**os** pian**o**-pian**os**

Nouns that end in **–y** and are preceded by a consonant drop their y and take **–ies** **Exception: 'monies,'** which is a legal term	baby- babies lady-ladies pony-ponies, etc.
If, however, the noun is **preceded by a vowel** we just add an **–s**	toy - toys boy-boys day-day, etc.
Nouns that end in **–f** or **–fe** drop the ending –f or –fe and **take –ves** to form their plural:	knife-knives leaf-leaves life-lives scarf-scarves self-selves shelf-shelves thief-thieves wife -wives
There are **some nouns**, however, **ending in –f** or **–fe** that take **-s** to form their plural:	belief-beliefs cliff-cliffs chef-chefs chief-chiefs dwarf-dwarfs handkerchief-handkerchiefs proof-proofs roof-roofs

Some nouns have irregular plural forms:	**man - men woman - women mouce- mice ox-oxen louce- lice**
Some nouns have the same plural form as their singular form. **Some of these verbs end in s, others describe some birds, animals and fish:**	deer, fish, salmon, headquarters, means, news, pecies, series, sheep, trout, etc.

UNCOUNTABLE NOUNS

Uncountable nouns **do not have a plural form.** They cannot be counted and therefore **are not used with a/an, many, or a number. Some, any, much, no, a lot of etc, are possible with uncountable nouns. The verb used with uncountable nouns is singular.**

Uncountable nouns are not used with numbers or a/an because they cannot be counted: ☞	Students should not **chew gum in class.**
For a **general meaning no article is used** with uncountable nouns: ☞	**Chewing gum** is not allowed in the classroom.
For a **specific meaning** the **article "the"** can be used with uncountable nouns: ☞	**I swallowed the gum** I was chewing.
The verb that we use with uncountable nouns **is singular** because uncountable nouns do not have a plural form: ☞	**My hair is** short and curly. **English is** my favourite subject. **The furniture** in her house **is** stunning. Your **money is** on the table. **Meningitis** can be treated if **it is diagnosed** on time.

Many times we use words of quantity like **some, any, no, (a) little, much with** uncountable nouns:☞	Can I borrow **some money** from you? Do you have **some/any money**? Can I have **some water** please? James doesn't want **any wine.** I have **a little time** if you feel like chatting.
If we want to count uncountable nouns **we use a pair of scissors, pance, jeans, a glass of milk, a loaf of bread, a cup of tea, a jar of jam, a bar of chocolate, a lump of sugar, a slice of cheese:**☞	I bought two really nice pairs of pants on sale. I bought three cartons of milk.

Helen Boubouli   **Grammar Genie**

List of uncountable nouns

Substances: oxygen, flour, bacon, beer, food, lunch, dinner, supper, coffee, tea, butter, pasta, air, grapefruit, gum, ham, milk, sugar, tea, water, wine, breakfast, alcohol.

Most diseases: chickenpox, flu, measles, mumps, polio, pneumonia, meningitis, rheumatism, Aids, Sars, headache, cold.

All sports: basketball, baseball, tennis, volleyball, hockey, cycling, canoeing, rugby, cricket.

Nouns ending in ing: boxing, shopping, jogging, swimming, hunting, running, sightseeing, etc

Languages: English, French, Spanish, Portuguese, Japanese, Chinese etc.

Academic courses: chemistry, computer science, history, geography, Ancient Greek, Modern Greek science, literature, physics, mathematics (maths),

Abstract nouns: love, peace, happiness, truth, advice, thunder, lightning, etc.

More uncountable nouns: progress, money, litter, garbage, trash, rubbish, luggage, baggage, mail, news, work, hair, traffic, transport, knowledge, etc.

Countable and uncountable nouns with a difference in meaning: "company," "paper"

uncountable	countable
Your company means the world to me.	My father owns a company that is in financial crisis.
Can you keep me some company tonight?	I own 50% of a company that recycles paper.
You are good company.	Some companies are closing down due to the financial crisis.
Do you have some paper for the printer?	Can you get me a paper (the newspaper) when you go out.

Note: there are some uncountable nouns that are sometimes used as countable nouns: coffee, tea, beer, wine, etc.

Uncountable nouns⮂	Used as countable nouns
Can I have **some beer?**	I would like **a beer** please?
Iwould like **some coffee.**	I think I'll have **a coffee** too.
	We would like **two coffees** please?

Plural collective nouns

There are **some nouns** that **only take a plural verb** even if we are talking about one item: **binoculars, braces, glasses, jeans, outskirts, pants, pajamas, spectacles, stairs, scissors, shorts, statistics, tights, trousers, tweezers, etc.**	My trousers **need** to be taken in. Where **are** the scissors?
A pair of +plural nouns can also be used with plural collective nouns that consist of two parts. The **verb** in this case can be **singular:** I bought a really nice **pair of jeans** the other day. I need **a new pair of glasses.** or Can you get me **a pair of scissors,** please? **The new pair of shorts** I bought **is** fabulous.	✓I bought **some/a pair of** really nice jeans the other day. ✓I need **some/a pair** of new glasses. ☒Can you get me a scissors please? ✓Can you get me **some/a pair of** scissors please? ✓The new **shorts** I bought **are** fabulous. ✓The **new pair of shorts** I bought **is** fabulous.
To talk about nationalities when referring to groups of **people (the Spanish, the British, the Welsh, the Irish, etc.)**	**The British** are known for their punctuality. **The greeks** are known to be very hospitable.

QUANTIFIERS

A few vs few
A little vs little

A few/few ⮕ used with plural countable nouns.
A little/little ⮕ used with uncountable nouns

I have a few questions to ask you.	(=some)	I have some questions to ask you.
I have few questions to ask you.	(=not many)	I don't have many questions to ask you.
I have a little time for you.	(=some)	I have some time for you.
I have little time for you today.	(not much)	I don't have much time for you today.

A lot of/much/many

A lot of ⮕ for interrogative and affirmative sentences with both countable and uncountable nouns

I have a lot of money.

Does he have a lot of money?

A lot of people came to see us.

much ➲ for interrogative and negative sentences with uncountable nouns

How much (money) did you spend today?

I don't have much money.

How much time do we have left?

many ➲ for **affirmative, interrogative** and **negative countable plural nouns**

Many **people** attended the lecture.

How many **cars** do you own?

I don't know many **people** here.

Both/both of

Both+plural nouns

Both stories were true.

Both kids are mine.

Both of + my/your/his/her/its/our/their/the + plural nouns

Both of the stories were true.

Both of the kids are mine.

Some ⭗

Some ⭗ used with plural countable and uncountable nouns:

in affirmative sentences

There are some people waiting for you.

There's some food on the table.

I have been up since 5 o'clock. I need some sleep.

in interrogative sentences, requests or offers.

Do we have some money for the theatre?

Would you like some coffee?

Please stay and have some tea with us.

Someone, Somebody, Something and Somewhere are used in affirmative and interrogative sentences, requests or offers:

You're hiding something from me, aren't you?

You know **something?**

Why don't we go somewhere and have fun tonight.

I met someone really nice.

Helen Boubouli   **Grammar Genie**

Somebody/someone/ anybody/anyone are used with singular verbs:

Someone wants to talk to you.

Is anyone here?

Has anyone seen my keys?

Any ⊃

Any⊃used with plural countable and uncountable nouns:

in negative sentences

I don't know **any** people here.

I don't have **any** free time.

in interrogative sentences

Do you have **any** free time?

Have you seen **any** good films lately?

in positive sentences after if

If **anyone** is late for class again, they will not be allowed to take the test.

in positive sentences

You can do **anything** you like.

You can go **anywhere** you like.

You can **see anyone** you choose.

Derivatives: **Anyone, Anybody, Anything** and **Anywhere** are used in negative and interrogative sentences.

Have you had **anything** to eat yet?

I haven't gone **anywhere** all weekend.

Any, anybody, anyone are used with singular verbs:

Is anybody coming with us?

I don't know **anybody** who **doesn't like** being pampered.

Is there **any** milk in the fridge?

Any, anyone, anybody, anything and **anywhere** are used with negative words (hardly, scarcely, never, rarely, seldom, etc):

I **hardly go anywhere** any more.

Hardly anybody showed up for the lecture.

dom talk to anyone here.

Helen Boubouli **Gramm*ar* Geni**e

The adverbs hardly, rarely, seldom, barely, scarcely, never, have a **negative meaning** and therefore, are not used with negative verbs since we cannot have two negative words in one sentence:

I **hadly go out**(= I don't go out much)

I **rarely see** him(=I don't see him often)

No ➲

No ➲used with plural countable and uncountable nouns:
in affirmative sentences with a negative meaning

I **have no** money. (=I don't have any money.)

I **speak no** foreign languages. (=I don't speak any foreign languages.)

Derivatives: **no one, nobody, nothing** and **nowhere** are also used in **affirmative sentences with a negative** meaning(the verb in the sentence is not negative):

I **know nothing** about what happened.(=I don't know anything about what happened.)

We **have been nowhere** the last five days. (=We haven't been anywhere the last five days.)

The adverbs **hardly, rarely, seldom, barely, scarcely, never,** have a **negative meaning** and therefore, are **not used with derivatives of no** since we **cannot have two negative words in one sentence**. Instead we use **hardly, rarely, seldom, barely, scarcely** + any, anyone, anybody, anything, anywhere):

I hardly have **any** money.(= I have very little money.)

Hardly **anyone** came to see us.(=Very few people came to see us.)

I hardly know **anybody** here.(=I know very few people here.)

I hardly **ever** go out anymore.(=I rarely go out.)

The words **nobody/ no one** are used with **affirmative singular verbs**:

No one informs me about anything in this house.

Nobody likes to work hard, but most of us have to. (People don't like to work hard, ...)

The lesson is boring. **Nobody pays** attention. (The lesson is boring. The students don't pay any attention.)

GERUND

Forms of the gerund
We form the **gerund** by adding **ing** to the verb:

I don't like play**ing** cards.

Use of the gerund

We use a gerund as the subject of a sentence:

Cycling helps me keep fit.

> We use **not+gerund** to form a negative gerund:
> **Not talking** to me won't help you solve your problem.

as the object of a sentence:

I really enjoy **writing.**

I don't enjoy **writing.**

after all prepositions:

He left **without saying** goodbye.

He succeeded **by trying** hard.

after possessive adjectives or object pronouns:

I look forward to **his/him coming.**

Go(come) +	**jogging**	He **goes jogging** for half an hour every day.
	shopping	I only **go shopping** for clothes during sales
	sightseeing	When I travel abroad I like **to go sightseeing** more than anything else.
	mountaineering	**Going mountaineering** is my favourite past time activity.
	fishing	Bill likes **to go fishing** once in a while.
	sailing	**Going sailing** in the summer is Ruth's hobby.
	clubbing	Every Saturday Tonia **goes clubbing** with her friends.
	swimming	How often does Veronica **go swimming?**

I suggest **your/you working** a little harder for this exam.

Helen Boubouli　　　　　　**Grammar Genie**

after genitive case:

John denied **Helen's cheating** in the test.

after nouns:

Did you forget your **mother** telling you not to go outside?

after the verb "go"+certain expressions used to talk about certain **sports and activities**:

after the expressions:

look forward to, be busy, be interested in, there's no point in, it's no use, what's the use of, can't help, can't stand, feel like, have fun, waste time/money, be used to, get used to, etc.

We **look forward to** seeing you.

I will be **busy studying** for my exams all week.

Be used to +ing ⊃ present habit
Be used to + noun

I'm used to drinking tea.

I'm used to tea.

I'm used to eating healthy food.

Get used to+ ing ⊃ try to get into the habit of doing something or try to become used to something
Get used to +noun

I'm trying to get used to waking up early.
(=I'm not used to waking up early, but I'm trying to become used to waking up early.)

 I can't get used to the cold weather in America.

I got used to my new English teacher.
(=I wasn't used to my new English teacher in the beginning but now I am.)

after the following verbs:

involve	appreciate	avoid
appreciate	avoid	**celebrate**
comprehend	imagine	**risk**
deny	delay	**detest**
regret	suggest	**spend**
dislike	discuss	**enjoy**
escape,	admit (to)	**escape**
forgive	like	**miss**

166

Helen Boubouli   **Gr**a**mm**a**r Geni**e

THE INFINITIVE

The full infinitive is used with:

"it" as the subject of a sentence+adjective: **it's important, it's necessary, nice, etc.**

It is important **to understand** what I'm saying.

It is a wise decision **to save your** money.

It's nice to see you again.

be+adjective:**(nice, sorry, happy etc.)**

I am happy **to see** you again.

I'm sorry **to see** you go.

after **the following verbs:**

agree	**seem**	beg
decide	**invite**	hope
remind	**promise**	refuse
tell	**try**	offer
want	**would like**	would love
prefer	**plan**	advise, etc.

too/enough+adjective:

It was **too cold** for **me to go** out.

167

adjective+ enough + to do something:

It **wasn't warm enough** for me **to go** out.

"in order to" and "so as to" to express purpose:

He studied hard **in order to do** well on the test.

He studied hard **so as to do** well on the test.

"it's time":

It's time **to go** to sleep kids.

It's time **to go** home.

It's time**(for you) to do** your homework

Helen Boubouli **Grammar Genie**

BARE INFINITIVE

The bare infinitive is used with:

modals (may, might, must, should, shall, would, will, can, could)

You **should** work less.

would rather/would sooner, had better

We'd better tell her the truth.
(=We should tell her the truth.)

I would rather/would sooner watch a comedy.
(present & future reference)
(=I prefer to watch a comedy.)

it's important, it's necessary:

Is it necessary **to attend** this lecture?

It is important **to understand** what you have to do in case of emergency.

let :

The parents sometimes **let** their kids **stay up** late on week ends. ⮕active voice

In passive voice the verb **"allow" +full infinitive" is used instead of "let":**

The kids are sometimes **allowed to stay up** late on week ends. ⮕passive voice

help ⮕both a bare or full infinitive are used in active voice with no change in meaning, while **in passive voice only a full infinitive is possible:**

Pauline helped Mary **(to)tidy** her room. ⮕active voice

Mary was helped **to tidy** her room. ⮕passive voice

make⮕a bare infinitive is used in active voice, while in passive voice we use a full infinitive.

The teacher made us **stay** after school. ⮕active voice

We were made **to stay** after school. ⮕passive voice

With **make, help, hear, feel and see** we use **bare infinitive in active voice** and **full infinitive in passive voice:**

Active voice	Passive voice
Mrs. Jones **makes her children go** to bed early.	Mrs. Jones' children **are made to go** to bed early.
We **heard you lie** to your parents.	You **were heard to lie** to your parents.
I **helped you lift** the box.	You **were helped to** lift the box.
The neighbours **saw you come** home drunk.	You **were seen to come** home drunk.

Let becomes allow in passive voice:

My boss **let** me **have** the day off. (active voice)

I was **allowed to have** the day off. (passive voice)

RELATIVE CLAUSES
Defining relative clauses
Relative pronouns used in defining relative clauses:

Relative pronouns

people	who/that
objects/animals	which/that
possessions	whose

Relative adverbs

place	where
time	when
reason	why

Who/that is used for people:

This is the guy **who** I was talking about.

Which is used for things and animals:

This is the house **(which)** I wanted to buy.

Where is used for places:

This is the place **where** I live.

The house **where** I grew up going to be demolished.

"That" can be used for people animals and things to replace who, whom, which, where, in defining relative clauses:

This is the guy (**who/that)** I was talking about.

When is used for time:

Do you remember the day **(when)** we first went out?

A defining relative clause gives important information about a person, thing or place and therefore cannot be separated by a comma from the main clause:

This is the girl **who/that** won the game.

The woman **who/that** is standing by the door is our English teacher.

Note: the relative pronoun **"that"** can be used to replace **who, whom, or which in defining clauses.**

In defining relative clauses when the relative pronoun is the object of the relative clause, it can be omitted:

This is the guy **(who/that**) Michael was telling you about.

This is the house **(which/that**) they robbed.

Note: The **relative pronoun is** an **object pronoun** if it is **followed by a noun, or subject pronou**n instead of a verb:

This is the new car **(which/that)** I bought.**(object pronoun)**

Note: The **relative pronoun** is a **subject pronoun** if it is the **subject of the verb:**

This is the girl **who/that** did really well on the test.**(subject pronoun)**

When the relative pronoun is the subject of the relative clause, **it can not be omitted:**

This is the girl **who/that** did really well on the test.

This is the house **which/that** was robbed.

The relative pronoun can be omitted only in defining relative clauses **where it is the object of the relative clause:**

This is the new car **(which/that)** I bought. **(object pronoun)**

This is the girl **(who/that)** I was talking to. **(object pronoun)**

This is the girl **who/that** did really well on the test.**(subject pronoun)**

> **Whose** is used both for people and things followed by a noun to show possession, **replacing his, her, its, their:**

This is the couple **whose** house was robbed.(=their house was robbed)

Why/that

The reason **(why/that)** I'm late is because there was a traffic jam.

Tell me the reason **(why/that)** you are not coming.

Non-defining relative clauses

A non-defining clause gives extra information, about a person or thing, which is not necessary in understanding the meaning of a sentence. It can be separated from the main clause by a comma without causing any confusion:

My grandparents**, who** are retired, live in the countryside.

That house, **whose** roof was blown away by the wind, used to be beautiful.

Note: the relative pronoun **"that"** is not used to replace who, whom or which in non-defining clauses.

✓Maria, **who** is my sister's best friend, has invited us to her birthday party.

✗Maria, **that** is my sister's best friend, has invited us to her birthday party.

The relative pronoun cannot be omitted in non-defining relative clauses even if it refers to the object of the relative clause:

I advised him to try to seem more assertive, **which** I think was what contributed to his being hired.

Note: Relative pronouns used in non-defining relative clauses: **who, which, most of whom, which, whose**

Helen Boubouli   **Grammar Genie**

MODAL VERBS

Modal verbs are special verbs that **give extra information about the main verb** that comes after the modal verb:

You **must tell** me the truth.

You **should see** a doctor.

You **should sleep** more.

All modal verbs except the verb "ought to" are followed by bare infinitive:

You **ought to** tell me the truth.

You **ought to** see a doctor.

He **must** tell me the truth.

Modal verbs **do not take "s" in the third person** singular:

She **should** see a doctor.

He **should** sleep more.

He **can** speak three languages.

Questions are formed by inverting modal verb and subject:

Should she see a doctor?

Should he sleep more?

Can he speak more languages?

Negations are formed by inserting **"not" after the modal verb:**

He **must not** tell me the truth.

She **should not** see a doctor.

He **should not** sleep more.

He **can not** speak three languages.

Modal verbs and auxiliary verbs are used to form short answers:

Yes, you should.

No, you can't.

Yes, we must.

No, you needn't.

No, I won't.

Yes, I do.

Yes I am.

When we use modal verbs present, and past, are expressed with their corresponding infinitives:

PRESENT INFINITIVE	do
He must tell the truth	
PERFECT INFINITIVE	have done
He must have told the truth.	

Helen Bouboubli   **Gr**a**mm**ar Geni**e**

may/might	request permission, perhaps	May I use your pen? John may get mad if you don't tell him the truth.
must	affirmative logical deduction, assumption	You **must** be sick. You look pale.
	affirmative obligation, necessity	You **must** see a doctor immediately!
musn't	negative obligation, necessity	**You mustn't eat junk food.**
should	advice	He (should) follow the instructions. you (should) take the next flight home.
ought to	advice	I ought to call my parents.
will	future reference	I will talk to him as soon as I can. They will

		probably be late again.
	future prediction	There will be rain tonight in the north of the country. They will probably be late again.
	decision made on the spot	I'll turn on the air conditioning. It's hot in here.
shall	**future reference** although used on rare occasions	I shall not be able to come.
	asking for advice although used rarely.	Where shall we go for dinner?
	"Should "is used more often rather than "shall"in question tags (small questions at the end of a sentence used to ask for confirmation to affirmative and	Lets go to the movies, shall we?

		negative sentences.)	
can	ability in the present or future permission	I **can help** you with the house work, if you'd like. You **can go**. Class is dismissed.
could	polite requests	**Could I have** a glass of water, please?
	ability in the past	When he was 5 **he could speak** three languages.
can't/couldn't	lack of ability	I **couldn't fix** the leaky faucet so I called the plumber.
	negative deduction, assumption	He **can't be** thirty. He looks over fifty.

"Can" and "could" have no infinitive form and no tenses other than present with "can" and past with "could." We use **"be able to"** when we want to use other tenses.

| I (can)am able to | I (could)was able to | I have been able to | I will be able to | I will have been able to |

"needn't" VS "didn't need to"

need to	necessity	You need to go.
needn't	lack of necessity (you did something although it wasn't necessary)	John and Mary called to say they were not coming. **I needn't have cooked dinner.**(=I had already cooked dinner before I found out that they were not coming.)
didn't need to	lack of necessity (it wasn't necessary and you didn't do it)	John and Mary called to say they were not coming. **I didn't need to cook dinner.**(=I found out that they were not coming, so I didn't cook dinner.)

"would"

"would"	used in 2ⁿᵈ and 3ʳᵈ conditionals	If he were more qualified, **he would be** eligible for the job. If he had gone to college, **he would have had** better job prospects.
	used as the past form of **"will"** in reported speech	You promised you **would not be** late.
	used to express repetition in the past	**When I was a kid,** I would wake up **very early on Sunday morning to watch cartoons.**
	polite requests	**Would you help** me lift this box, please?

Although the following verbs behave like modal verbs, they are not:

have to	**necessity obligation but not as strong as** "must"	**You** have to go **to school.**
	certainty	That **has to be** Steve. They said he's tall and blond.
have got to	necessity, obligation but not as strong as **"must"**	**I have got to finish** writing this grammar book by Christmas.
	certainty	The robbers **have got to have known** where the money was hidden.
had better	strong advice, threats	It's getting late. **You'd better go** now before it gets dark. **You'd better start** studying harder or you'll flunk your test tomorrow.

be to=for something that will happen or is scheduled to happen

All **the students are to pass** an oral exam at the end of the course.

Helen Boubouli **Grammar Genie**

Modal infinitives

When we use modal verbs Present, past, and future are expressed with their corresponding infinitives:

Present infinitive	do
He must tell the truth	
Present continuous infinitive	be doing
He must be telling the truth.	
Perfect infinitive	have done
He must have told the truth.	
Perfect continuous infinitive	have been doing
He must have been telling the truth.	

Tenses corresponding with the infinitives
{Present Infinitive/Present Continuous Infinitive/Perfect Infinitive/ Perfect Continuous Infinitive}

Simple Present:	Present infinitive
He **is** probably at work.	He **must be** at work. (positive deduction).
He **is** probably not at work.	He **can't be** at work.(negative deduction)
Simple Future	
He **will have to** work.	He **must work.** (affirmative obligation)
He **will not have to** work.	He **must not work.** (negative obligation)
Present/Future Continuous:	Present continuous infinitive:
Maybe **he's working**	He **might be working.**
Maybe **he will be working.**	
Simple Past/Present Perfect/ Past Perfect:	Perfect infinitive:
Maybe he **worked.**	He **might have worked.**
Maybe he **has worked.**	
Maybe he **had worked.**	
Past Continuous /Present Perfect Continuous /Past Perfect Continuous:	Perfect continuous infinitive:

Helen Boubouli   **Grammar Genie**

He **was probably working.**	
He **has probably been working.**	He **must have been working.**
He **had probably been working.**	

Helping verbs or auxiliary verbs

The following verbs can be used both as helping verbs(auxiliary verbs) and as main verbs:

do, be, have, will, shall

When used as helping verbs, they are always followed by a main verb:

Do you **speak** English?

I am **reading** the paper at the moment.

Have you finished studying?

Will you come to see us this weekend?

When used as helping verbs:

"Do" "does" are used to form the interrogative, and **"don't" "doesn't"** to form the negative in the simple present. **"Did"** is used to form the interrogative, and didn't is used to form the negative in the simple past.

Do you speak English?

I **don't** like horror films.

Did you read your mail?

"**Am**" "**is**" "**are**" are used with the present participle to form present continuous, "**be**" is used with the present participle before modal verbs to form continuous types (present continuous, past, future continuous, and future perfect continuous, and with the past participle to form passive voice. "**Was**" " **were**" are used with the present participle to form past continuous.

I **am not going** to work today.

He **must be** sleeping.

I **will not be visiting** my parents this Christmas.

I **was hoping** you would call.

"**Have**" is used with the past participle to form perfect tenses (present perfect, present perfect continuous, past perfect, past perfect continuous, future perfect and future perfect continuous.)

Have you seen any good films lately?

The kids **have ben lying** lately.

The house **has been broken** into.

"**Will**" is used with a bare infinitive to form future tenses.

Will you be coming to see me this week end?

Helen Boubouli   **Gramm**a**r Geni**e

Irregular Verbs

VERBS (INFINITIVE)	SIMPLE PAST	PAST PARTICIPLE
be	was	been
bear	bore	born (e)
beat	beat	beaten
become	bacame	become
begin	began	begun
bite	bit	bitten
blow	blew	blown
break	broke	broken
bring	brought	brought
build	built	built
burn	burnt (burned)	burnt (burned)
burst	burst	burst
buy	bought	bought
can	could	(be able to)
catch	caught	caught
choose	chose	chosen
come	came	come
cost	cost	cost
cut	cut	cut
deal	dealt	dealt
dig	dug	dug
do	did	done
draw	drew	drawn

dream	dreamt (dreamed)	dreamt (dreamed)
drink	drank	drunk
drive	drove	driven
eat	ate	eaten
fall	fell	fallen
feed	fed	fed
feel	felt	felt
fight	fought	fought
find	found	found
fly	flew	flown
forbid	forbade	forbidden
forget	forgot	forgotten
forgive	forgave	forgiven
freeze	froze	frozen
get	got	got
give	gave	given
go	went	gone
grow	grew	grown
hang	hung (hanged)	hung (hanged)
have	had	had
hear	heard	heard
hide	hid	hidden
hit	hit	hit
hold	held	held
hurt	hurt	hurt
keep	kept	kept

know	knew	known
lay	laid	laid
lead	led	led
learn	learnt (learned)	learnt (learned)
leave	left	left
lend	lent	lent
let	let	let
lie	lay	lain
light	lit	lit
lose	lost	lost
make	made	made
mean	meant	meant
meet	met	met
pay	paid	paid
put	put	put
read	read	read
ride	rode	ridden
ring	rang	rung
rise	rose	risen
run	ran	run
say	said	said
see	saw	seen
sell	sold	sold
send	sent	sent
set	set	set
sew	sewed	sewn
shake	shook	shaken

shine	shone	shone
shoot	shot	shot
show	showed	shown
shut	shut	shut
sing	sang	sung
sit	sat	sat
sleep	slept	slept
smell	smelt (smelled)	smelt (smelled)
speak	spoke	spoken
spell	spelt (spelled)	spelt (spelled)
spend	spent	spent
stand	stood	stood
steal	stole	stolen
stick	stuck	stuck
sting	stung	stung
swear	swore	sworn
sweep	swept	swept
swim	swam	swum
take	took	taken
teach	taught	taught
tear	tore	torn
tell	told	told
think	thought	thought
throw	threw	thrown
understand	understood	understood
wake	woke	woken

Helen Boubouli   **Grammar Genie**

wear	wore	worn
win	won	won
write	wrote	written